THE

PILLARS OF TRUTH:

A Series of

SERMONS ON THE DECALOGUE.

By E. O. HAVEN, D.D., LL.D.,
PRESIDENT OF THE UNIVERSITY OF MICHIGAN.

New York:
PUBLISHED BY CARLTON & PORTER,
SUNDAY-SCHOOL UNION, 200 MULBERRY-STREET.

Entered according to Act of Congress, in the year 1866,

BY CARLTON & PORTER,

in the Clerk's Office of the District Court of the United States for the Southern District of New-York.

PREFACE.

THE following Discourses were delivered before the students of the University of Michigan, in the College Chapel, on Sabbath afternoons, and are now published without alteration. After the close of the series the Young Men's Christian Association of the University adopted the following resolution:

"*Resolved*, That we have listened with great interest and profit to the series of discourses on the Ten Commandments, delivered by Rev. Dr. HAVEN, President of the University, on Sabbath afternoons, and would respectfully suggest to him the propriety of having them published in the form of a book."

The thought of printing them had not previously been entertained by the author; and having concluded to assent to the suggestion, it has not been thought advisable to give a more extended examination to the subject, though the Decalogue is practically inexhaustible, and a thorough treatise upon it would be a complete moral philosophy.

It will be seen that the author has not aimed at a florid style, but rather to express the most valuable truth in a few simple and direct words. In this way he has found that the careful attention of listeners is secured, and he trusts that those who have sufficient interest in the subject to read the discourses will find them promotive of that thought and faith essential to the best and highest life.

UNIVERSITY OF MICHIGAN,
ANN ARBOR, *July*, 1866.

CONTENTS.

THE

PILLARS OF TRUTH.

THE FIRST COMMANDMENT.

Worship only God.

THOU SHALT HAVE NO OTHER GODS BEFORE ME.—Exodus xx, 3.

Is any man among us ever inclined to break this commandment? Has not that part of the world called Christian outgrown all disposition to break it? If so, to explain it is only to gratify curiosity, and practically superfluous.

It is not so. Not only is every one of the Ten Commandments binding upon all men, every one is also often broken by persons who have received Christian instruction. The Decalogue is God's grand compendium of moral philosophy. Whoever obeys it in letter and spirit is a perfect man. A young man once said to Jesus, "All these have I kept from my youth up!" He must have entertained a very high estimation of his own character to have made such an assertion honestly. I doubt not that he was a man of excellent moral character, and yet he certainly could not have "known himself" to have made so preposterous a claim. Probably careful self-examination, aided by the illumination of the Divine Spirit, would have shown him that he had violated all of them. But it is not necessary to break all the Ten Commandments severally to be guilty of breaking them all; for "he that keepeth the whole law, and offendeth in one point," says an apostle, "is guilty of all." How is that? Why, simply, if a man deliberately breaks any one of a code of laws he sets at defiance the authority of them all as much as though he should break them all severally. It is the spirit, not the outward act, that God looks at.

Let us now investigate this commandment carefully: "Thou shalt have no other gods before me."

1. This question immediately arises: What is it to *have* a god?

Observe, the lawgiver does not assert, There is no other god besides me. It may seem to some that this would have been a better way of expressing the true meaning of the commandment; but so it did not seem to the Giver of the law.

He does not say, Thou shalt not *believe* that there are any other gods before or besides me. Had he done so an atheist might have kept the commandment easily; but I think we shall find it is not so easy for an atheist to keep the commandment as it is written.

What then is meant by *having* a god? Is it meant that we must not have any images or idols, and worship them? That is forbidden in the *second* commandment. If the first and second commandments mean the same thing, one or the other is superfluous, which we cannot acknowledge.

Is it meant that a man must not believe that there are spiritual beings, or gods, besides God, superior to man, which he might worship if he thought best? Certainly not, for the Bible teaches that doctrine, and Christians do believe it.

What then is meant, the question recurs, by *having* gods?

Observe, that "having" is purely subjective; it applies to the person that *has*, and does not necessarily affect the person or thing *had*. I may have a house to-day. I may sell it, and not have it to-morrow; but the house remains the same. It is I that change, not the property.

There must, then, be a certain condition of a man when he *has* God, and another condition when he *has* other gods before the true God; and these are the only two conditions mentioned or implied in this commandment, and perhaps these are the only two possible conditions to an active responsible human being.

Observe, again, that neither of these conditions of a man can possibly affect the existence of the true God, or of the false gods. My *having* God does not cause him to be. My not having him does not cause him not to be; my having false gods does not cause them to be, and my not having them does not cause them not to be. They either are or are not, and their existence is a matter entirely independent of me; but this *having* is a *command*, which I can break or keep as I will. Of course I cannot, by my will, affect the existence of God or gods; but I can have or not have gods before the true God, as I determine.

The question comes back then with force, What is this voluntary act of a man, by which he can have, or not have, either God or false gods?

The conclusion is inevitable, that this commandment applies only to *man*, and is designed to apply to every *man*, and has no reference or direct application to God or to false gods. It is a commandment to me from God: "*Thou* shalt have no other gods before me."

Of course, then, there is immediately ruled out of this commandment every sense of the word which implies compulsion or necessity. There is a sense in which every man *must* have God, and must have him before every other being. God is, and none but a fool says in his heart, "no

God." The most stupid sensualist on earth, who grovels only in brutish life, is created and sustained by God. He *has* God in one sense of the words, and must *have* him, and cannot possibly have any other being in his place, simply because it is impossible that any other being should be in his place.

But this sense of the word is excluded, because in a *commandment* the word cannot bear this meaning. It is a thing not to be commanded or denied because from the nature of things it must be. All finite beings, including Satan, *have* God in this sense; for God made them, and none other can take the place of God to them.

The question then is narrowed down to this: What is it to *have* God *voluntarily?*

The Hebrew language is not rich in words. It is in this respect a kind of child language, endeavoring to express all thoughts by a few vocables; and a literal translation of the Hebrew Scriptures into English is therefore likely to be misunderstood.

To *have*, in the Bible, often means not only to possess, but to use and employ, just as an intelligent and upright person might be expected to do. Thus to have God implies that we should be affected toward God, and by our knowledge of him, just precisely as we ought to be; and to have other gods before him, implies that we allow some other beings, or powers, or ideas, or beliefs, to stand in our minds where God ought to stand, and to affect us as God ought to affect us.

Now it seems to me superfluous to argue that we ought to entertain a reverential regard for God's approval, so that in all matters a belief in his approval would be paramount to all other influences in affecting our decision. Thousands of questions arise in every man's life, when, if he is a true worshiper of God, this consideration turns the balance and settles the decision. The questions may be, Shall I choose this occupation or that? Shall I enlist in the army? Shall I study a profession? Shall I abide at home, or emigrate to another part of the world? Shall I devote myself to making money? Shall I cultivate my mind? Even questions of less magnitude, as, Shall I embark in this special enterprise? Shall I make this particular decision? How can a man be said to *have* God, if he does not allow his views of what God will approve or disapprove to affect, yea, even where there is a suspense, to decide these questions? To such a man, I suppose, God is; but just now, so far as he is concerned, God might as well not be. He is not allowed to exert the proper authority of God. Man abuses his little day of trial, his short season of independence and discipline, to such an extent as actually to shut out God from his narrow territory, and thus he has no God.

But "nature abhors a vacuum," and if a man will not allow his views of what God approves or disapproves to decide such questions, then some other power, either personal or ideal, will step in and usurp God's place.

Suppose, for instance, a man decides all questions of conduct and character simply with regard to making money. Why, then, how evident is it that his god is mammon, and we all remember the words of Christ: "Ye cannot serve God and mammon." Now it matters not that this man is never profane perhaps; that he may be correct and moral in outward deportment; that he is even in the Church: if mammon decides such questions for him instead of God, he *has* mammon instead of God. His soul worships mammon instead of God.

Substitute for mammon, pleasure; then pleasure becomes god. Substitute any particular gratification, it usurps the place of God. There are even now in this country worshipers of Bacchus, of Venus, of Mars, of Apollo, and of the whole family of the divinities in the Pantheon of old. The Hindoos have many thousands of gods; no more, however, than the rivals of the true God, even in Christian lands.

Now this element of the word "have" needs careful attention not to be misunderstood. To have God implies not merely a regard for him, but even a supreme, absorbing regard for him.

If, therefore, anything but God is allowed to *control* a man, that other thing becomes a rival to God—in the words of our text, another god. That other thing may probably be allowed to influence a man in a subordinate degree, but it must not control the man.

There is a great difference between controlling a man, and exerting a proper subordinate influence over a man. Many powers, agencies, or thoughts are excellent servants, but bad masters. We abominate the worship of the sun, but we appreciate it as the great material source of power and life. The old Egyptians worshiped bulls; it does not follow that we should not use them to plow our fields.

All those passions of which I have spoken—the love of wealth, ambition, the love of knowledge—are good: good as subordinate motive powers; good as servants, not good as gods.

A man needs and should desire to be controlled—must be controlled, steadied, shaped, and charactered—by some power from without; that is, by a motive or feeling that he can separate from himself, and discard if he will, or allow to act if he will. That motive or power is to him a god.

God himself is voluntarily controlled by his

own law. He does not live capriciously. "Every good gift, every perfect gift, cometh down from the *Father* of lights, *with whom is no variableness, neither shadow of turning.*" He chooses not to change.

Now a man is either a weathercock or a slave, or he is a voluntary servant; and voluntary service of a high principle, or of God, is freedom.

The most essential element in the idea of God is authority based on superior power, and therefore the good-will of that being is eminently desirable. Almost all heathens, ancient and modern, regard the beings that they call gods as capricious and imperfect. Some are cruel, and delight in pain; some are foolish, and must be flattered; some are passionate, and must be indulged; and so the poor victims of superstition are frightened into sacrifices, degrading services and usages, and pagan slavery.

Now I have thought that any man who indulges a faith that leads to like results must have other gods before God, even though he is not generally regarded as an idolater.

A man may violate the first commandment and be in name a worshiper of the true God.

Suppose, for instance, that the priests of Brahma should meet in convention to-day, and agree that hereafter the English word God should be substituted in all places for the Hindoo word Brahma, so that hereafter they, instead of being called worshipers of Brahma, should be called worshipers of God. Would the mere change of name change their character? Suppose, on the other hand, a missionary to China, in translating the Bible into Chinese, falls into a verbal error through ignorance, and uses instead of the proper word for God a wrong word, which really means an idol, and himself offers up a prayer, as he thinks, to God, though he really uses a name appropriated to an idol, would that mistake vitiate the prayer? Does God care whether he is called

"Jehovah, Jove, or Lord,"

if he is only worshiped in spirit and truth?

Evidently not. Names are nothing except as they are significant.

If this be so, the question whether a man breaks the first commandment or not, whether he really has other gods before God, is translated altogether from the sphere of words into the realm of thoughts. It is not a matter of signs and ceremonies, but a matter of ideas. It is a subject which grows deeper and deeper in significance as men's minds are disciplined and informed. It is a matter that the infant cannot comprehend at all, that is very dimly seen and little understood by the child, and by all old persons who in mind never rise out of the childhood plane of development; but to those of extended and careful and thorough thought, how rich it is!

Emancipated from thraldom to terms and forms and creeds and customs, it becomes an intellectual and moral question, to be considered in the serene atmosphere of truth, What is it to *have* God, the true God of the universe? What is it to have some phantom, some hideous caricature of God, or some actual inferior intelligence, on God's throne in the soul?

How fitting, then, is it that this commandment should be the first in place, as it seems to be the first in comprehensiveness and power. A lawyer once asked Jesus, "Master, which is the first and the greatest commandment?" Jesus in reply simply changed our first commandment from a negative to a positive form, and then expressed in full language what is properly included in *have* when applying to God. Instead of saying, "Thou shalt not have other gods," he said, Thou shalt do thus and so. And instead of using the obscure and too comprehensive word "have," he employed a rich paraphrase: "Thou shalt love the Lord thy God with all thy heart, with all thy soul, with all thy strength."

This comprehends our entire duty to God. This stands at the very threshold of piety, and this is so rich in meaning as to embrace our entire duty.

Now in the further consideration of this subject we may consider all men as divided into three classes, as follows:

I. Those who do not seem to entertain any definite or controlling ideas of God whatever.

II. Those who entertain radically unscriptural, and therefore erroneous, ideas of God.

III. Those who cherish and obey radically scriptural, and therefore correct, ideas of God.

I. The most of human beings are unfortunately very ignorant of God, and many are not concerned to know anything about him. Our country, probably, has less of this kind of population than any other in the world. We cannot find many here, as among the peasantry and manufacturing population of some European countries, who would say on inquiry that they never heard of Jesus Christ; but we have many who have never read the Bible, never exercised any continuous thought whatever about the serious problems of spiritual life and eternity. "God is not in all their thoughts." They eat, drink, marry, and are given in marriage, and when death approaches sometimes go through with a little flurry of religious excitement, and sometimes not, and then pass away.

Were all the world like them there would be no Sabbath, no temples of worship, no songs of praise, no prayer, no profound philosophic thought, for metaphysicians are always interested in religious questions; and I am constrained to think that other science would languish, institutions of learning would die out, the bonds of good society would loosen, evil passions would riot without restraint, and the earth would become desolate and a ruin.

These men are generally regarded as practical atheists; some of them are and some of them are not idolaters. They all, however, worship something else besides the true God. Those who neglect God are often very superstitious. They believe in witchcraft, or in the rappings of spirits, or in lucky and unlucky days, or in fate, or in some other phantom of a diseased and corrupt mind, instead of the infinitely wise, just, and good moral Governor of the universe. Some passion often becomes their god.

II. The second class of men are those who entertain radically wrong notions of God.

This, of course, embraces all genuine idolaters, men who break the second commandment as well as the first. The earth is full of idolatry. Men have not liked to retain God in their knowledge and have degenerated into savages.

It embraces also those in Christian lands who worship a false god in the name of the true one. Those who believe the Divine One to be unjust or partial; to be capricious, or changeable without reason; to be implacable, and fond of inflicting pain; to be void of justice, so as to allow a sinner to escape punishment simply because it is painful to witness suffering; to be destitute of knowledge or interest in his own creatures, so as not to regard prayer; to be enslaved, so as to be a mere Fate or Necessity, or to be bound by anything but by his own love and right and wisdom; all these men really have another god before God. They use the same name, it is true, and entertain some right notions; but the grand fact remains unchanged—they violate the first of the Ten Commandments.

The consequences have been awful. Sin in Churches, in professed Christendom, heresies, variances, jealousies, ecclesiastical ambitions and intolerance, persecutions and cruelties, have all sprung from this prolific fountain.

How strong ought to be the impression on every young mind: your entire religious character may be ruined by incorrect views of God.

III. The third class are those who entertain scriptural and therefore correct views of God.

No man is, I presume, absolutely faultless in this regard. The subject is so incomprehensible, and educational influences are so diverse, that active minds cannot perfectly agree upon their conception of God. In fine, an active mind is continually changing its own views as it learns new facts and receives new experiences, and becomes more and more familiar with the sacred writings.

Some have said that a man's idea of God is simply a magnified conception of himself. They seem to think that a David must think of God as an infinite David; a Nero as an infinite Nero; a Franklin as an infinite Franklin; and, in fact, every one as himself, with all his deformities, infinitely magnified.

Now this is absurd. And yet there is some truth in it; for an absurdity, you are aware, is always a distorted truth. It is true that man could not know God if he was not created in God's image. We can understand God only from ourselves. Every attribute of God corresponds with a faculty in man, or he could not conceive of it.

But it is possible for us, from ourselves as a foundation, aided by supernatural instruction, to obtain an idea of a *perfect man*, free from our own deformities and inherent disposition to evil, and through that, with the idea of infinity, to rise to a conception of God.

No man, therefore, can see God as he is without having a correct idea of a good man; and none but a pure man can rise to that idea. Therefore Christ said in his great sermon,

"Blessed are the pure in heart, *for they shall see God.*" None but the pure in heart can see God; and they see him in proportion to their purity.

Man's own soul is the lens through which he looks to God. But this spiritual lens, like the lens of the eye, can be rectified and strengthened only by use. It is only by a persevering, prayerful life of virtue, that the soul can be so ennobled as to choose the true God for a Ruler.

Whoever does this is a man; a full, complete, well-rounded man. He is in sympathy with the universe because he is at one with its Maker. To him good is positive and eternal; evil is exceptional, repulsive, and contemned. If betrayed into sin he despises it, and finds no peace till he is delivered from it and has reason to hope that it is forgiven.

Such a man appreciates and trusts in Christ; for Christ reveals God to man as the Saviour of sinners, by granting them forgiveness when they abandon sin.

How much more, then, does this commandment mean to us than it did to the Israelites who first heard it! They understood simply that they were to have no other god—no Isis, or Moloch, or Dagon, or other idol—but only to worship Jehovah. We understand that any ambition, hope, or purpose, if allowed to control us, is a rival to him; and that to have him really is to be fully a righteous and a religious man.

This is a characteristic of the richest portions of the Bible—to be inexhaustible in resources. They are like the sun, whose rays served the world for sight for ages, but afterward were found by science to have a chemical power, and a medical power, and a photographic power, and may yet be found to have many other powers. So the Bible has instruction in it not yet discovered.

Have any of us other gods above God? If so, the end of our false worship will be disappointment and disgrace. It matters not how common it is, how many examples of it there are, or how pleasant for a season; that is the end.

Have any of us God on the throne of the soul? We are safe. We cannot be permanently disappointed. We shall surely succeed.

II.

THE FIRST COMMANDMENT.

Believe in God.

THOU SHALT HAVE NO OTHER GODS BEFORE ME.—Exodus xx, 3.

THIS implies that we must have or believe in God. The Bible nowhere adduces any arguments to prove the existence of God, or of man, or of the earth, or stars, or the wind, or the sea, or of spirits good and evil, or even of a soul in man's body. Strange as it may appear to mere logicians and theoretical theologians, the Bible assumes the existence of all these, and proceeds to talk about them, and reason upon them, as though no man of good sense would call their existence in question.

Now it is worthy of notice that no man ever learned of the existence of God by argumentation, nor of the existence of any of the leading beings or powers in the universe. We do not induct children into a belief in their own existence by a syllogism, or by a combination of premises ending with a therefore. How strange and amusing a sight it would be to see a mother endeavoring by a dialectical and scientific process to convince a child four years old of the existence of the sun. She would first, I suppose, lay down the proposition or axiom that "no effect takes place without a cause," and illustrate it at some length. She would then call the child's attention to the mists of the morning, the clouds of the afternoon, the budding of the trees, the shadows cast by opaque bodies, and a thousand other optical, and chemical, and perhaps vital phenomena; and finally be prepared to arrive scientifically at the conclusion, "There is, there must be, therefore, a great source of light and heat, that we may call the sun." But probably by this time the child would be asleep, or very much puzzled by his mother's learned conversation; and, even though he had his father's full understanding, his conviction of the existence of the sun would not be half so strong and vivid from all this logic, as he could obtain by just lifting his eyes up at once at the great luminary as he rises in the morning, and seeing it once for himself. As the people well say, "Seeing is believing." There is profound philosophy in that remark: "Seeing is believing."

Now the existence of ourselves, of external nature, and of some of the prime qualities of both, we learn actually by "seeing." Perception and consciousness are both of them processes of seeing. By the one we see certain existences and facts without us, by the other certain existences and facts within us, as a part of us; and neither of them can we doubt without insanity, and neither of them can we prove or disprove by what is commonly called a process of argumentation, or by the logical process of arriving at truth and detecting error. If you undertake to prove logically the existence of the earth, you may possibly make a man doubt it; you certainly cannot make him believe it any more strongly than before. Precisely so with the existence of himself, with the existence of the fact that there is a connection described by the words cause and effect, that there are such qualities as right and wrong, virtue and vice, unity and diversity, time and space, the finite and the infinite. These thoughts and beliefs come to us, or grow up in us, or are a part of us, so that, although we may not think of them for years, or perhaps may never think of them until some other person suggests them to us, when we do once learn of them we cannot seriously doubt of their existence, and we can never forget them again.

These are the ultimate facts, primary truths, absolute existences, uncreated seeds of thought, all that we know or can know about which is, that they are, and must be, whether we think of them or not.

Now I class our belief in the existence of God among these primary truths believed by the human mind, according to its own constitution, without argument.

But there are objections to this statement.

1. It is often maintained, with a great show of learning, that the religion of man has gradually developed and increased from a thin stratum of fear, and a superstitious dread of the personified forces of nature, through fetichism, and the worship of beasts, to a coarser idolatry, embracing human sacrifices, and thus on to a refined mythology, like that of the Hindoos and the Greeks, till finally monotheism became the natural belief. In other words, there was a time when no man believed in one God; but as men advance and become sufficiently enlightened, all men will believe in one God; and perhaps the next step will be to deny his existence!

This is a very beautiful theory, that has often been encased in the choicest style of very elegant writers, and it seems a pity to disturb it; but there is one objection to it that honesty compels me to present: it has no basis of fact to rest upon. The most careful scrutinizer of the past has never yet been able to find one division of the human family, one race, one nation, one little tribe, one family, who were known once to have been idolaters, and afterward to have arisen to a conception of the one true God by their own mental growth, through the process of argumentation.

Not only is there no fact to support the theory, but unhappily for it there are many very striking facts against it. For instance, the oldest nations of the earth, according to all the written and traditional records of the times, beyond which exact history is silent, in their earliest days seem already to have believed in one God and worshiped him; and as their history comes down, it is found that idolatry commences and is developed as a product of later times!

Now, in these days of the Baconian philosophy, it is exceedingly offensive to be called upon to believe a theory because it is beautiful, when it is not confirmed by facts, and all the facts that do relate to it oppose it.

It is inexcusable for men to attempt to prove, by *à priori* or deductive reasoning, what *must* have been the origin of a practice or thing, when we have the history to show what its origin actually was. Men may with propriety invent hypotheses to account for the pyramids of Egypt, because we know nothing about their origin; but they must not invent a theory to account for the origin of St. Peter's Church in Rome, or St. Paul's in London, for the origin of these we know. They may dogmatize, if they will, about the mounds in North America; but they must not dogmatize about Bunker Hill Monument or the Erie Canal, for their history we know. Geologists may theorize about the origin of the Niagara Falls, but they must not endeavor to throw a mist about the origin of the Niagara Suspension Bridge.

We do not assume to have full daily or even annual and unbroken records to trace the history of a belief in one God, from this time backward to Adam or Noah; but this we do assert: the earliest historical records contain the doctrine; they contain it more plainly and abundantly than later records; and no facts exist to indicate that the idea was a gradual indigenous growth in any age or among any people.

A modern writer, who is far more noted for his undigested learning than for his logic, Mr. Buckle, gives us one phase of the hypothesis, that religion is an effect of development and civilization rather than a superior controlling cause, as follows. Speaking of the Hebrews, he says:

"Thus it was that the doctrine of one God, taught to the Hebrews of old, remained for many centuries altogether inoperative. The people to whom it was addressed had not yet emerged from barbarism; they were, therefore, unable to raise their minds to so elevated a conception. Like all other barbarians, they craved after a religion which would feed their credulity with incessant wonders; and which, instead of abstracting the Deity to a single essence, would multiply their gods till they covered every field and swarmed in every forest. This is the idolatry which is the natural fruit of ignorance; and this it is to which the Hebrews were perpetually recurring. Notwithstanding the most severe and unremitting punishments, they at every opportunity abandoned that pure theism which their minds were too backward to receive, and relapsed into superstitions which they could more easily understand, and into the worship of the golden calf and the adoration of the brazen serpent. Now and in this age of the world they have long ceased to do these things. And why? . . . To what possible circumstance can this subsequent change be ascribed, except to the simple fact that the Hebrews, like all other people, as they advanced in civilization, began to abstract and refine their religion, and, despising the old worship of many gods, thus, by slow degress, elevated their minds to that steady perception of One Great Cause, which at an earlier period it had been vainly attempted to impress upon them."*

Here an ingenious effort is made to produce a conviction precisely opposite to the truth. The idea of God among the Hebrews was not a gradual growth. It was suddenly communi-

*History of Civilization in England. By Henry Thomas Buckle. Volume I. Pp. 236, 237. London: John W. Parker & Son, West Strand, 1857.

cated to them through Abraham their father. There is no evidence that they lost it in Egypt, though slaves and ignorant. They relapsed into idolatry occasionally for several generations; but the idolatry into which they relapsed *did not imply the denial of the existence* of one supreme God. They became idolaters, not because they were ignorant, but because they were surrounded by idolaters, and because by uniting with them they could throw off the restraints of the Ten Commandments, and indulge in immorality. Men are wicked now without being atheists. The two tribes never yielded to this temptation after their captivity, though they were still what Buckle would term ignorant and undeveloped. How was it during the history of the Maccabees? Were they superior in mental culture to the Macedonians? How in the time of Christ? Was Josephus superior as a philosopher to Tacitus? the Pharisees to the Stoics? He must indeed be blind, or must manufacture his own *facts* as well as theories, who does not see that the very central idea of the old Hebrew nation was ONE GOD; and that though they were unfaithful to it for a time, afterward, through trials and discipline, without any perceptible advance in mental culture, and while still inferior in this to many heathen around them, they finally became profound believers in God, and performed their mission in that regard well.

Facts all seem to point to the conclusion that the world has never, since history began, been destitute of a belief in God—one uncreated, independent Creator and Ruler. Occasionally parts of nations have forgotten it; the worship of demons, or of beings supposed to be superior to man, but inferior, of course, to God, has sometimes so degraded the mind as to cause the *populace* to forget God; but there have always been some who have preserved the doctrine, and few indeed have been the adult human beings that have not in some form heard and thought of it. This idea is one of the common possessions of humanity. Every language has its word for it; every human being has some idea of what that word means.

2. But still another practical objection may be urged to the proposition that a belief in God is one of those truths that the mind has without argument, and from its own nature believes.

It may be said that men who are not taught the doctrine do not believe it. The deaf and dumb are appealed to. Some of the most interesting questions relating to the mind may be investigated by observing the mental operations of those persons who are deprived of one or more of the senses. They are obliged to act more slowly than other men, and therefore we can see the process; or we can learn how much and how little we acquire through the senses of which they are deprived. Now of all of the deaf and dumb that have been taught to think and communicate thought, from the days of the Abbe Sicard until now—and they number thousands—not one has been found who says that he was conscious of any idea of God, one or many, till after he had received the idea from his teacher. Hundreds have been directly asked the question, and the reply is always in substance the same: "I did not think of God." Some express their former fears and anxieties and strange feelings when they went to church and saw what they afterward learned was worship; and some were amazed at attending funerals to see a person lying motionless and buried; but none of these things gave them an idea of God. Many of them had an idea of immortality, or rather no definite idea of death; but none had ever thought of God.

This fact seems at first to be equally opposed both to the theory that we arrive at our knowledge of God from the observation of evidence of power, design, and intelligence in the works of nature, and also to the theory that we obtain our idea of God from our own souls, or that it is born in us. If we obtain it from argument, why are not some of these deaf and dumb persons intelligent and acute enough to find out God by argument before they are taught the language of signs? If the idea is born within us, why is it not born in them?

To this we can only say that the fact alone is not conclusive proof of any position on the question at issue. It does, however, indicate that all of us are indebted for our first thoughts about God to *information received from others.* This is undoubtedly as a matter of fact true. Probably all who listen to me now received their first ideas of God from their mother, or from some one who took the mother's place. It was while in your mother's lap, or just learning to walk, when that feeble intellect was just putting forth the tender buds of promise, and your limited vocabulary of words was almost constantly employed in asking questions, that you first heard the awful word, GOD. How blessed a thing it is that mothers frequently are pious, at least in the presence of their little children, for it evinces a fearful hardness of heart and insensibility to love, for a mother to fail to give all possible good influence to the tender mind of her child. And thus it comes to pass that nearly all children, at least in a Christian land, learn of God from their mothers. Often, too, the father aids, and he can only aid in this work. The holy instinct of a mother's love leads her to reject with scorn the cold and wicked philosophy of Rousseau, who would fain have all children, like the deaf and dumb, kept entirely ignorant of God and Christ, and heaven and hell, and right and wrong, and everything religious, till they were adults, in order that they might not be prejudiced! This is like forbidding children to eat anything till they are adults, for fear they might violate the laws of health or injure their constitutions! It is about as well to starve physically as spiritually; the mind as well as body can be developed only by use.

This communication of the idea of God from parents to children corresponds exactly with the practical directions of the Bible. The Hebrews were positively commanded and required to teach their children about God. It is equally the duty of parents under the Christian dispensation. The Christian mother or father who does not see to it that his child has correct and full ideas of God is guilty of great neglect and sin.

But how does this fact bear on the proposition that the idea of God is an intuition of the mind, originated or sustained by the soul itself, and not dependent for its reception or its force upon argumentation? Simply thus far only. It is found that the child, when the idea is once presented, naturally grasps and holds upon it, and never forgets it. If it was the result of an argument, he might forget it; many would certainly forget the logical process that leads to it, and their belief in it would thus be weakened. But this is not the fact. Men never forget the idea of God. No man naturally disbelieves it. Every man, every child, naturally feels it to be true. Reason may by and by confirm it; knowledge will modify it; his idea of the Divine One will change very much, but his mind always tends to embrace and cling to it. We pronounce it thus an original product of the mind itself, though it needs the suggestion of some other mind, at least usually, to bring it into the range of consciousness.*

Now this is true of other intuitions, such as space, time, eternity. There are many adults, doubtless, who have never thought of space, boundless, empty space, in which all things that are or can be can exist, and yet have just as much of it as though there was not a single thing created. I say many have never thought of this mysterious infinite space, but after they

* This principle is recognized by all good mental philosophers. It is stated by nearly all. Perhaps a better statement of it cannot be found than that of Cicero in his De Oratore, lib. iii, cap. 3. "Nam neque tam est acris acies in naturis hominum, et ingeniis, ut res tantas quisquam, nisi monstratus, passit videre; neque tanta tamen in rebus obscuritas, ut eas non penitus acri vir ingenio cernat, si modo adspexerit:" For there is not sufficient acuteness in the nature or intellect of man to perceive these truths unless they are *told to him;* nor yet is there such a kind of obscurity about these truths that any man of good sense can fail at once to perceive them, if once his attention is called to them.

have once thought of it they never can forget it; they never can deny its existence. This, therefore, we call an intuition. It is a thought revealed, not by argumentation, but by simple presentation. It grows out of our own soul, though few even think of it until it is suggested. If there are two violins near each other, and a string on one is made to vibrate and sound, the corresponding string on the other also vibrates in unison with it. Now if that second violin only had a consciousness and a will, it might prolong and increase that sympathetic vibration into a loud, joyous life. This is precisely the way that souls act and react on each other in the awakening of these intuitions. They are silent till aroused; but when aroused they act spontaneously. The older one, having been stimulated into action by a predecessor, in turn stimulates another, and each has a self-sustaining, moving power of its own. Thus do we learn to think of God. I believe that it would be of great advantage to all well-educated men to understand thoroughly the basis on which true religious convictions rest, and therefore I propose to examine this subject a little more closely. If it was my object only to amuse, or even interest, I might choose a subject less abstruse and more rhetorical; but, young men, you will hereafter be appealed to as liberally educated men; you certainly ought to scrutinize carefully the foundations of faith; and if you have a faith and hope, be ready to give a reason for it; and if you have not a faith and hope, be ready to give a satisactory reason for that fact if you can.

The doctrine that our idea of God is one of the primary convictions or knowledges of the human mind, needing only to be suggested to be at once spontaneously comprehended and felt, is confirmed by the fact that several other ideas are of precisely the same character. The idea of cause and effect, of right and wrong, of unity and diversity, are of this kind. Also there is in man's mind a spontaneous power of entertaining such views of the external world, and of himself, as requires the use of lauguage. Language, therefore, is not a gradual growth any more than religion. You are aware that precisely the same diverse theories on the origin of language have been entertained as on the origin of religion. Some have imagined that men once were so ignorant and brutal that they uttered only inarticulate cries, like the chatterings of monkeys, the brumming of oxen, the neighing of horses, and the barking of dogs. Finally some genius among these human dogs first blundered upon articulation, and began to assign names to things. Afterward another genius invented verbs, and then another prefixes and suffixes, another adjectives and adverbs, till finally the euphonious and flexible speech of a refined people was reached.

Now the objection to this beautiful theory is that it has no known basis of fact, and what facts we have bear against it. The earliest known languages are rich in vocabulary, complicated in structure, philosophical and refined in their laws of variation. Almost all savages have a language too good for themselves to understand, and which certainly could not have been invented by more savage predecessors. They indicate deterioration and not progress in the people.

Herodotus, in his gossiping account of his travels in Syria, relates an experiment which was tried there by a curious philosopher at least five hundred years before Christ. This relation, by the way, proves that the theory of inductive reasoning was understood not only before Bacon, but even before Aristotle, Plato, and Socrates. But though understood, it was not extensively and properly practiced, the great mistake of the ancients being a too great reliance upon the power of their own minds in deductive reasoning, and not giving a sufficient attention to known facts. The relation of Herodotus is as follows:

Before the reign of their king Psammetichus the Egyptians esteemed themselves the most ancient of the human race; but that king investigated the matter, and decided that the Phrygians were older. His method was to select two infants and have them nursed by a shepherd without any opportunity of hearing a word uttered, and it was found that both of them when two years old first pronounced the word *bekos*, which in the Phrygian language meant *bread.**

The prince philosopher did not observe that the word *bekos* might have been an imperfect imitation of the bleating of a sheep, which the little ones often had heard.

Rev. Dr. Horace Bushnell, in his chapter on language, introductory to the argument of his work entitled "God in Christ," gives us a description of a singular fact bearing on this subject that is said to have happened in Connecticut a few years ago. He says:

"A very distinguished artisan, whose name is familiar to the country at large, himself a scholar and a keen philosophic observer, had a pair of twin boys who were drawn to each other with such a mysterious and truly congenital fondness as to be totally occupied with each other, and thus to make little or no progress in learning the language of the family. Meantime they were constantly talking with each other in a language constructed between them, which no one but themselves could understand. In this

* See Herodotus, book ii, chap. 2.

language they conversed at their plays as freely as men at their business, and in a manner that indicated the most perfect intelligence between them. At an early age one of them died; and with him died, never to be spoken again, what, beyond any reason for doubt, was the root of a new original diversity of human speech, a new tongue." *

This is very strongly stated, but it is not sufficiently exact to be of any scientific value. Dr. Bushnell did not himself see or hear the two children speak their new language. The father may have been deceived by his parental fondness. Besides, it is strange that no other members of the family are represented as having learned a word of the new speech. Had the little ones spoken Chinese or Hebrew the other members of the family would have learned it. Though there may have been some foundation for the narrative, it is too isolated and unsupported and unnatural to base any reasoning upon it alone.

Dr. Bushnell adds:

"Indeed, to believe that any two human beings, shut up wholly to each other, to live together until they are of mature age, would not construct

* God in Christ. Three Discourses delivered at New Haven, Cambridge, and Andover, with a Preliminary Dissertation on Language. By Horace Bushnell. Pp. 17, 18. Hartford: Brown & Parsons. 1849.

a language, is equivalent, in my estimation, to a denial of their proper humanity."

That also is a strong statement, but it is simply an opinion. So to suppose that a single human being of good sense and intellect would grow up to adult age without an idea of a Creator, would seem at first to impugn his proper humanity, and yet many such human beings have grown up. We are little aware how much we owe to education, and especially education by example. The most complicated processes seem simple after they are once understood. How simple a process is writing, and yet the world of men lived centuries without an alphabet. Men, perhaps, will by and by wonder that the world could have stood six thousand years without a magnetic telegraph!

In process of time, perhaps, many of these questions may be tested by actual experiment, on a sufficiently large scale to ascertain the truth. In the mean time we should not too confidently theorize upon them.

How many of these central ideas of the human soul—ideas of the reason, as the transcendentalists call them—were actually reached by man without any stimulus from a higher being or an instructor, cannot now be ascertained. If man was originally created by God by a direct fiat, as both reason and the Bible teach, he cannot have been thrust into this world as an adult infant; but he must have had aroused in him those primitive energies of the soul which give him character, among which are an appreciation of cause and effect, a feeling of the difference between right and wrong, and an idea of God.

All facts seem to indicate that man when created was taught at once also to speak. The outward world, to be understood, requires the use of language. Subjectively in man there is a nature that is fitted to the use of language. This is no more true of the vocal apparatus than of the intellect and whole soul. And though it may be doubtful whether man, being wholly destitute of language, would not live even for centuries without originating one, yet it is evident that, once given to him, he is fitted to receive, appreciate, and use it, and that he can never forget to use speech. Man can degenerate from civilization to barbarism. He can lose the use of fire, the arts of metallurgy and of carpentry, the restraints of law and decency; but should he sink so low as to forget the use of language and the idea of God, he would not be far from death, and the race would soon become extinct. That some tribes have sunk into such savagism cannot be denied; but that any have unaided risen from it to monotheism and refinement, cannot be shown.

My belief is that it is as natural for man to

believe in God as it is to exercise speech, or to make music, or to organize government. While we can imagine man to live for ages without either, we have no reason to believe that he did, and if the practices or thoughts were once reached they would never be forgotten.

This view should be guarded from the extreme statement that an idea of God is an instinct. By instinct is meant an impulse or feeling in an animal which prompts him to act in a wise and proper course, without understanding the reason of his action and without education from others. Thus birds that have never seen any of their own kind will build their nests without instruction, according to the habits of their particular species. Insects hatched from the egg, without the company of other insects, will not only provide for themselves, but make ample and exactly the required provision for their posterity; all of which shows that they act without instruction and without reason. The honey-bee makes his hexagonal cells for the honey, it being precisely of that form in which a given amount of material, like wax, could be made to hold the greatest possible amount of substance, like honey. That this was the required form for such a purpose could be approximately shown by experiment, but could not be demonstrated mathematically without a use of the differential calculus, a science which we can scarcely allow that the honey-bee comprehends.

Now we do not claim that man's conception of God is an instinct.

Man has few instincts, and those few are mostly brought into exercise when he is in infancy and helpless. Man depends on education and reason. But education cannot work without material, and reason requires her fundamental and acknowledged principles. So soon as man can exercise the senses, and understand what he feels, the mind, by its internal resources, begins to suggest to him the great central principles of mathematical and mental and moral science. As from time to time, mostly by the aid of some teacher, he is taught to observe his own mental actions, these principles become to him acknowledged, established, appreciated, and believed. They cannot be doubted without trouble; they cannot be denied without remorse; and if any persist in a verbal denial of them, others are convinced that the denial is only superficial and verbal, or that some abnormal influence has temporarily clouded the reason of the unhappy skeptics.

Such is the common belief of man in God.

If my position is correct, we see the impropriety of those labored arguments often found in theological works to *prove* the existence of God. The very title and aim of the arguments are offensive. When Bishop Watson presented a copy of his work, entitled "An Apology for the Bible," to George III., the king remarked, "I did not know that the Bible needed an apology." He was not aware that the bishop had used the word in its Greek and not in its English sense, meaning an argument for the Bible; but his criticism was a good one. The title of the book in English was unfortunate. The office of observation and argument is to *confirm* our belief in God, to show his attributes, his nature, his will, and not to *prove* his existence, as though that was a thing to be established by a process of ratiocination, or reached by a long and laborious study, like a formula in calculus.

God! the universe is full of him. His voice is in the running brook, the whispering breeze, the roaring ocean. His beauty is seen in the stars, the firmament, the ocean, the dew-drop. Nothing is too small to show his skill, too vast to speak his power.

What is the practical use of this subject? Simply this: to make or deepen the impression that not to think of God is both a folly and a crime. It suppresses and benumbs and destroys our highest faculties. It shuts us out from the largest and best enjoyments. It belittles us and imbrutes us. But to think of God as he is —omnipotent, omnipresent, holy, indignant at sin, loving goodness, personal, and interested in us—is the substance of a right life. "The fear of the Lord is the beginning of wisdom."

Only through Christ and in him can we obtain a full and correct view of God, and only by repentance and abandonment of sin are we prepared to love God; and thus there is revealed to us a richness of meaning in his holy word that otherwise we cannot see.

III.

THE SECOND COMMANDMENT.

Idolatry.

THOU SHALT NOT MAKE UNTO THEE ANY GRAVEN IMAGE, OR ANY LIKENESS OF ANYTHING THAT IS IN HEAVEN ABOVE, OR THAT IS IN THE EARTH BENEATH, OR THAT IS IN THE WATER UNDER THE EARTH: THOU SHALT NOT BOW DOWN THYSELF TO THEM, NOR SERVE THEM; FOR I THE LORD THY GOD AM A JEALOUS GOD, VISITING THE INIQUITY OF THE FATHERS UPON THEIR CHILDREN UNTO THE THIRD AND FOURTH GENERATION OF THEM THAT HATE ME; AND SHOWING MERCY UNTO THOUSANDS OF THEM THAT LOVE ME, AND KEEP MY COMMANDMENTS.—Exodus xx, 4–6.

ONE half of the world and more are the worshipers of idols. If we estimate the population of the globe to be one thousand millions, at least five hundred millions are provided with images, to which they offer religious worship with more or less earnestness. Indeed the Bible seems to intimate, and other history seems to corroborate the opinion, that once all the world were idolaters. In the days of Abraham, who besides him was not accustomed to worship idols? And for a long time who besides his descendants were not idolaters? And when Elijah thought that he was alone, but it was afterward supernaturally revealed to him that there were "seven thousand men that had not bowed their knees to Baal," how many more in all the world besides this seven thousand were there that did not bow the knee to some false god?

Indeed this is a statement in which all agree, whatever their opinions on other matters, infidel or Christian: once all the world was given to idolatry. If, then, we should subscribe to a favorite notion in America, that numerical majorities may decide moral questions; if we should adopt and approve the sophistical maxim of Vincentius, *Quod semper, quod ubique, quod ab omnibus*, "What is always, everywhere, and by all received," idolatry would even now be be voted the religion of this globe. It could to-day command not only a plurality, but an absolute majority of the votes. But inasmuch as it is wrong, we have reason to be encouraged, because now, for the first time, *nearly* half of the world are redeemed from the practice; and soon, we may hope, all idols everywhere will be flung to the moles and the bats, or be preserved in museums as specimens of the superstition of past ages.

I. I propose to inquire, first, *What is idolatry?* I mean idolatry proper, not figurative or imaginary, but the real thing.

And here allow me to remark explicitly, that I believe it to be the duty of a preacher on the Sabbath, above all men, to be candid, and just as entirely free from error as he can possibly be.

He should never consciously use a sophism, and never discolor the truth, even to do good. God's cause will always suffer in the end as the result of any degree of unfairness.

I cannot, then, paint idolatry, as a sin of the mind or heart, so black as some have drawn it. I cannot pronounce it so absurd as most of us from our childhood have been taught to consider it. I cannot regard some degrees and kinds of it so intrinsically wrong as many have pronounced it. If I had been brought up in China or India, and was not a Jew or a Mohammedan, I should have been an idolater. Many are idolaters innocently, and perhaps virtuously. Many who are real Christians, and are esteemed as Christians, innocently, through ignorance, practice a kind of idolatry. Idolatry is not a practice pronounced to be wrong by the common untaught conscience of all men, like murder or theft. If you hear of a tribe of men, or of an individual man, that professes to believe that murder is not wrong, you infer that that man is insane, or that tribe has perverted or lost their manhood, and are no more fair specimens of the common conscience than the aboriginal dirt-eaters of California are fair specimens of the taste of man for food. But when you hear of a tribe that they are idolaters, you do not deem it indicative of idiocy or insanity. We should never know idolatry to be wrong unless informed of the fact supernaturally, or unless we had thought out the fact by the severest logic; and therefore, till we should thus learn it, it would not be wrong for us, though of course in itself always wrong.

Idolatry is not so puerile and illogical as many now affect to consider it. It might be enough to say on this point that Socrates was an idolater; and if any man pronounces Socrates unwise or immoral, it is simply because he knows nothing, or very little about the subject. No man who believes that Socrates uttered the sentiments attributed to him, and lived the life related of him by his disciples—Plato, Aristotle, and Xenophon—can doubt that he was a wise and a good man; but he was an idolater. His last utterance was a request that a sacrifice which he had promised to the god Esculapius should be offered. Plato was a profound man, and Plato was an idolater. Aristotle was encyclopedical in knowledge, and constructed his vast information into systems of thinking of wonderful symmetry; and Aristotle was an idolater.

Nor must we be so arrogant as to suppose that there is no wisdom, and that there are no wise men, no skillful jurists, no profound legislators, no accomplished leaders, no strong and well-disciplined minds in China or Hindostan. Some of the Indian philosophy quite rivals the Greek in acumen and breadth. Some of the

Indian poetry is rich in thought and passion. And think you a population of two hundred millions of human beings could be supported and governed in the United States of America without learned and able statesmen, without scientific agriculture, without labor-saving machinery, without well-regulated industry, without high civilization? But if this would be the fact in America what must be the fact in China? It is preposterous pride and folly alone that would lead us to suppose ourselves superior to the Chinese in some of the most essential arts of life. Facts speak louder than words; and certainly in some facts they surpass us. But the Chinese are idolaters.

I. It becomes us, then, first to investigate the question,

WHAT IS IDOLATRY?

Some have taught that idolatry is the worship of an image, or images, with the belief that those images are God, the very God that made heaven and earth.

This is entirely an error. So stupid a human being probably never lived. It would indicate not only stupidity, but an entire perversion of the human intellect, to entertain such a proposition. Any man could more easily believe that he himself made the earth, sun, moon, and stars, than that any wooden or brazen image of his construction made the earth, sun, moon, and stars. No idolater ever conceived of so absurd a thought.

This mistaken idea of the nature of idolatry is easily accounted for. Idolaters were accustomed to talk about gods. We are accustomed to talk about God. Inasmuch as the word is the same, we fancy that they meant by gods what we mean by God. This is far from the truth.

By gods they usually meant mysterious powers above or superior in some respects to men, nevertheless interested in man; they conceived of them as persons, each occupying a portion of space; some larger, some smaller; some in society, some in solitude; some in certain localities, and interested particularly in certain peoples. Many of these gods, indeed, were believed to have been, and were originally, men, such as Hercules and Esculapius.

The people in those times were not accustomed to think closely on these subjects. They did not inquire into evidences and probabilities on questions of religion. These beings superior to men were talked of before the children from their infancy, and they could recollect no time when they did not believe in them. In their daily life they were constantly reminded of it. Was there a destructive storm? Some god or being a little or much superior to man brought it on, and sacrifices were offered to him to induce him to be favorable thereafter. Was there a famine, a deluge, a drought, a plague? The process was the same. All their domestic life was intermingled with ceremonies of connection with the gods.

But besides these intelligences the heathen believed in GOD ALMIGHTY as we do, and never attempted to make an image of him that fills heaven and earth.

Poets and imaginative writers among them invented stories about their gods and goddesses—those fancied beings little or much higher than men—their marriages and quarrels, their feasts and contests. These stories if uninteresting were soon forgotten; if interesting, were remembered and repeated, and soon came to be believed as facts by many of the people. Thus a god acquired a fixed character, and all the new stories about him were made to correspond with his established personality. Thus arose heathen mythology.

Ere long images were made to represent these gods. At first rude pictures, and blocks of wood and stone, uncouth and ugly; but in process of time, as sculpture advanced, through the demand for these images, they became more and more symmetrical and perfect, till in Greece, particularly, the most splendid and various statuary ever made represented their fancied gods and goddesses. The Egyptians and Hindoos never rose above ugliness in their statues, but both of them, in the architecture of their temples dedicated to the worship of their gods, surpassed all other nations in the magnitude and expense of their structures. The great temple of Diana at Ephesus, mentioned in the Bible, was an Asiatic edifice, the product of Asiatic mind and organized labor, though its oriental magnitude was in later times adorned with Grecian refinement. Though the Greeks called it one of the seven wonders of the world, because they never saw anything like it, yet I doubt whether in magnitude and expense it was equal to the temple of Belos in ancient Babylon, or to some temples now standing in Hindostan and used for idolatrous worship.

Idolatry in some countries has been attended by enormous expenditures of money, of labor, and even of life. Its temples, statuary, sacrificos, priesthood, have absorbed more of the energies of the people in some nations than even the efforts to obtain the necessaries of life. There is no accurate and comprehensive calculation upon this subject with which I am acquainted, but, undoubtedly, it will be investigated; and when so, the result will probably astonish the Christian world, and perhaps make the Church ashamed of its comparatively feeble efforts to honor the real God of the universe.

Our definition of idolatry is the following: Idolatry is the worship of any object, living or dead, natural or artificial, supposed to have power (or to represent some being that has power) to reward the worshiper. This includes the worship of men, such as the worship of the Grand Lama, in Thibet; the worship of the ghosts of dead men, such as, perhaps, the worship of Apollo, Esculapius, Hercules, and even Jupiter; the worship of the sun, moon, and stars, of rivers and mountains, and of all idols or images made to represent any fancied spiritual beings.

Almost everything in the heavens above and in the earth beneath and in the waters under the earth has been worshiped, from the sun to a pebble; from the moving firmament to an insignificant annual plant; from a man to the entrails of a dead beast. To us, educated with the open Bible, and enlightened by the severe natural and mathematical and historical science of modern times—science, in which no genuine idolaters of a low style of religion ever did or could excel without laying aside their superstitions—to us, no phenomena of human nature are so marvelous as some of the facts of idolatry.

We can understand how men might worship the sun, moon, and stars, before the revelations of the telescope and of geography and of mathematics, for they might fancy them alive or the representatives of living powers; we can understand how men might worship great men of past generations, like Washington or Columbus, for what is more natural than to suppose that Washington now as a spirit should watch over the United States, and Columbus over America? And even now millions of Christians pray to saints, which is idolatry. We can imagine that a statue, or a mountain, or a river might be worshiped, as representing an invisible demon or angel; but that men should worship a brother man, like the Lama, or a Roman emperor; that human beings should worship a cow, or cat, or a piece of broken glass, or a fragment of tin, only shows to what depths of ignorance and folly human beings can plunge. Still it may be better even to worship an insect or a stick than to worship nothing, for this degraded practice reveals the presence of an instinct which God has created, and which ought to be exercised; and which, when directed to the great Author of our being, exalts us into intimacy with Christ and into a fitness for heaven.

Idolatry then, in itself, is not so absurd as some have deemed it. If we were not divinely informed that it is wrong, and leads to evil, we might deem it reasonable, as it certainly is natural. But for the Bible, all the world would again become idolaters.

Having thus considered the nature of idolatry, we pass on to inquire,

II. WHAT RENDERS IDOLATRY SINFUL?

Idolatry is explicitly, uniformly, and repeatedly forbidden in the Bible. It is condemned alike by Judaism and Christianity. It is unequivocally and positively prohibited to all who receive the Bible. To those who know not its sinfulness it may be excused, for an inspired apostle said, when exposing its folly and wickedness, "The times of this ignorance God winked at, but now commandeth all men everywhere to repent," to change their thoughts and their actions on this subject, "for he hath appointed a day in which he will judge the world, by that man"—his Son Jesus Christ—"whom he hath ordained" to be the Judge of the world, "whereof he hath given us assurance in that he hath raised him from the dead."

In portraying the evils of idolatry we must not place the philosophy of man above the declaration of God. God's reasons, we may be sure, are the strongest reasons.

God's main reason, if I may be allowed the expression, the prime and only reason which God saw fit to write on the stony tablet of the Decalogue, is this: "*For I, the Lord thy God, am a jealous God,* visiting the iniquity of the fathers upon the children unto the third and fourth generation of them that hate me; and showing mercy unto thousands of them that love me and keep my commandments."

Now, friends, let us look at this awful divine assertion carefully, without prejudice, without shrinking, in the daylight of truth.

There is a God. Jehovah, the maker of all things, exists. He is not absent from any place. All men know that he exists, or should know it and feel it. How men came to know of the existence of God is stated in the Bible. In the earliest ages of history God revealed this truth to the first generation. And this truth is of such a character, it is so consonant with the human reason, it is so confirmed by the appearance of the result of wisdom and power in the world of matter and mind, that once given to man it cannot well be wholly lost. And, indeed, God has himself guarded against having it lost. The greatest purpose of the foundation and preservation of the Israelitish nation was to insure the world against the loss of a belief in God. All the great races of men have believed in God. All the leading languages have a particular term for the Divine One. The thinking men among idolaters generally have believed in the one God. The Egyptians, the Greeks, the Romans, the primitive men of Europe, the aborigines of America, all believed in God, though they were idolaters.

But we are taught in the Scriptures not only that there is one God, and only one, but that he is a Person. He is a Being of character and will, of pleasure and displeasure, of approval and disapproval, of action, of reward, and punishment. He is not a silent, passionless One, as some of the East Indian philosophers have foolishly imagined. He is not a great Fate, or blind Necessity, as some of the Greek philosophers vainly taught. He is not a mere Law, or infinite, unfeeling, unreasoning Power, as some modern naturalistic theists seem to suppose. He has the three great elements of a perfect mind—sensibilities, reason, will.

Now this must not be forgotten. Whoever denies it is no Christian. Whoever denies it dishonors God.

Observe, every faculty, every capability in man's soul is a representative of what exists in God. Man is finite, but finiteness is not a passion or faculty, it is only a limitation; but this finiteness subjects man to conditions that cannot exist in God. Evil passions in man are not intrinsically evil elements, but only good passions wrongly exercised. There is love in man and love in God; but man's love is often wrong, God's love is always right. There is anger in man and in God; but man's anger is often wrong in object and degree, God's anger is always right. This is true of all passions and of all modes of mental action.

Now God assures us in the text—which is a part of the Decalogue, God's own handwriting —that he is a JEALOUS GOD.

Jealousy is, therefore, sometimes right. The word translated jealous here is used in this form only to describe the displeasure and indignation of the Divine One, if he should be neglected, by his well-instructed people, for the worship of any other being. But words from the same root are used to exhibit displeasure at being neglected, indignation at seeing what one may justly claim conferred upon another.

God has created man with such faculties and energies that, if man is not perverted, he will love his Creator. God sees that it is wrong for a man to lavish on an idol the emotion due to himself. He therefore feels it to be a wrong. Knowingly done, it is an insult; unwittingly done, it is still an offense.

May we not illustrate this from our own nature? The father and mother have a claim to the love and respect of their child. If a child capriciously, or to obtain improper indulgence, forsakes his parents, neglects them, dishonors them, seeks a friend to honor and confide in, in some inferior, unworthy person, have not the parents a right to be jealous? Does not our purest, unsophisticated conscience approve the grief and the resentment of the father and the mother? But why? Has God given to a good human parent, created in his image, a passion not found in his infinite heart? "He that formed the eye, shall he not see? He that planted the ear, shall he not hear? He that teacheth knowledge, shall he not know?" He that has made you to exercise a good and righteous feeling, shall he not feel? Be assured there is not an emotion expressed by word, or gesture, or action, by poetry, oratory, or the imitative arts, the perfect prototype of which is not in the Infinite Heart; there is not a thought, a perception, a relation, a law, a truth, in the compass of human science, the unlimited source of which is not in the Infinite Mind. When, therefore, God asserts that we must not worship an image, because he is "a jealous God," he must mean that he desires our love and worship; he resents it as a wrong if we withhold it; he looks upon it as an insult if we bestow it upon any created thing.

How criminal, then, is idolatry! How ungrateful it is not to worship God!

Here I might naturally close this discourse, for this completes the most obvious practical instruction of the text; nevertheless careful examination shows that not only does the Divine One resent idolatry, but that in his infinite justice punishment follows. These words demand examination.

III. How does God "visit the iniquity of the fathers upon the children unto the third and fourth generation of them that hate him?"

Observe, this is spoken of idolaters; and also only of those idolaters who once knew God, but forsook his worship for idols.

This punishment may be what men would call *natural*, for God is the author of nature. If a man swallows poison he is punished by loss of life. God is the author of the effect. Nature is only growth; but this growth itself must have a living, personal cause, and that is God.

Now the natural effects of idolatry—the effects which God has appointed and brings about—are,

1. Pernicious to the mind. It degrades the intellect; it destroys the power of careful investigation. What is truly called science cannot flourish with idolatry. No heathen people have been noted for science. They have had literature and art, but their science is elementary, generally contemptible. Greek and Roman science was scarcely above contempt, wholly unworthy of the attainments of their great men in other branches of mental activity. And nearly all of their men who did investigate science, even to their limited extent, practically discarded idolatry during their active life. They became theists, or sole believers in one God, regarding idolatrous mythology as largely alle-

gorical or uncertain, and of more profit to the people than to them. Deism was a step upward for idolaters.

2. Idolatry belittles the soul. The human soul wants a perfect standard to aspire after. Deprived of this it is like an eagle with clipped wings, compelled to lie on the ground and to flounder in the mud. The tendency of an idolatrous people is always downward, never upward. There is no instance in the history of the world of an idolatrous people's rising up without missionary aid from abroad, throwing off their idols and becoming men. Infidel philosophy is continually prating about the gradual improvement of man; but when, on the Baconian system, we ask for an instance of a whole tribe rising from idolatry to theism, from savagism to civilization, without missionary aid, it is silent. No such instance was ever known. An idolatrous nation is like a man addicted to intemperance: there is little hope of either becoming sober. We say of an habitual drunkard, who always resolves after every fit of drunkenness that he will drink no more, but, nevertheless, returns again to his cups, Poor fellow, he is a ruined man. So God said of the Ten Tribes of Israel, five sixths of the descendants of the people who had first heard this Decalogue, after they had become idolaters, "Ephraim is joined to his idols: let him alone."

This downward tendency of idol worshipers is forcibly stated by the Apostle Paul in his Epistle to the Romans, many of whom had lately been rescued from it. "Because that," says he, "when they knew God, they glorified him not as God, neither were thankful; but became vain in their imaginations, and their foolish heart was darkened. Professing themselves to be wise, they became fools, and changed the glory of the incorruptible God into an image made like to corruptible man, and to birds, and four-footed beasts, and creeping things."

3. But another and severer punishment of idolatry is immorality. The heathen cannot maintain a high standard of morality. They have no written word. Their gods and goddesses are nothing but the conceptions of wicked men. They are peevish, avaricious, cruel, thieving, lustful, and if any of them have any goodness or virtue it is incomplete and deceptive; and those who worship them tend to become like them, only worse; for it is a well-known law of human nature, that imitators generally surpass their models in their faults and fall short of them in their excellences. Therefore in morality idolaters constantly tend to degenerate. All history confirms this proposition. The exceptions stand out glaringly as exceptions, and may easily be accounted for, and thus illustrate the rule.

The Apostle Paul, in his same letter to the

Romans, presented this subject with great fullness, from whose description we quote but a few words more: "And even as they did not like to retain God in their knowledge, God gave them over to a reprobate mind, to do those things which are not convenient; being filled with all unrighteousness, fornication, wickedness, covetousness, maliciousness; full of envy, murder, debate, deceit, malignity; whisperers, backbiters, haters of God, despiteful, proud, boasters, inventors of evil things, disobedient to parents, without understanding, covenant-breakers, without natural affection, implacable, unmerciful: who, knowing the judgment of God, that they which commit such things are worthy of death, not only do the same, but have pleasure in them that do them."

This terrible picture of the morals of heathenism is inspired. This picture we know to be true. That all idolaters are not alike degraded and polluted I acknowledge. This only shows the recuperative energies of the human soul, acted upon by God's Spirit, never absent from man. That some bright specimens of virtue occasionally present themselves is true, but they are only oases in the wilderness of death, only faint phosphorescent gleams in the ocean of desolation. Whole nations have perished in this maelstrom of hell. The long lost Ten Tribes of Israel, that theorists and geographers have sought so diligently on this little globe, where are they? Gone down into the idolater's grave, never to rise again till the judgment of the great day!

"Assyria, Greece, Rome, Carthage, where are they?" Echo answers, Where?

There are races now on earth inoculated with the virus of destruction beyond recovery. There is but one medicine competent to save them, and that they will not take, and some will perish, I fear, before they have the offer. This is the just judgment of Heaven upon those who do "not like to retain God in their knowledge."

But are there not some practical lessons in this for us? I answer, yes; and with one or two I close.

1. First, we ought earnestly to guard against idolatry ourselves. The first step is a neglect of the worship of God. It is easy to be irreligious; it is hard to be non-religious. It is unnatural to be inactive. We cannot without persistent violence smother a faculty of the soul. The hand will move; the feet will walk; the eyes will see; the ears will hear; the reason will inquire; the affections will fasten upon some object. The religious nature will act. In affliction, in distress, in disappointment, in extreme danger, the soul will pray. Let it be, then, to God. Cultivate the habit of it in youth,

in health, even now. Lay in a stock of good principles and of good habits. Thus guard against those "evil days in which you will have no pleasure in" the senses, or in the things of the earth. The only true safeguard against some insidious form of false worship is the worship of God.

2. These idolaters have a claim upon you. Some of you may yet be called to be missionaries to the heathen. Almost every college in the land has missionaries raising the banner of Christ before the gaze of those taught to worship idols. Already some of our alumni, of at least two branches of our university, are there; and some have fallen on the field where they pointed sinners to Christ, or have come home to die. Why may not others follow? Undoubtedly others will. It is the noblest field for faithful, self-denying men.

Remember, many of these idolaters now are not to blame. It was their fathers, not they, who "did not like to retain God in their knowledge." God hath yet much people among them. They are waiting to be instructed. The Macedonian cry is rising from many a district, "Come over and help us." Shall not the Church respond? Shall the nations perish, and their more favored brethren not lift a hand to save them? Shall half the world receive the Gospel, and that largely, through missionary efforts, and then shall the recreant sons and daughters of the Church let its banners trail in the dust, and the rising tides of darkness surge over the world? No. Forbid it, Heaven! Forbid it, men! In the name of the Bible societies, publishing annually millions of copies of the blessed Word, forbid it! In the name of the missionary societies of every vital part of the Christian Church, forbid it! In the name of the fallen martyrs, such as Schwartz and Henry Martyn and Fisk and Cox and Elliott and Judson and Collins, and a host of others, men and women of whom the world was not worthy, who have died among the poor heathen they went to bless, and over whose graves thousands converted from heathenism have wept, forbid it! It must not, shall not be. We will be interested in this work. The Church shall have its laborers, and the Church shall sustain them, till not a city, or village, or hamlet, or wandering tribe, or hut, or wigwam, or cave on the round earth, shall be found, where God the Father, Christ the Son, and the Holy Spirit, One Jehovah, shall not be known.

This hope has inspired Christians from the beginning. This faith makes Christianity not a "religion of sorrow," but of hope. Ancient literature looked backward to a fancied golden age; we look forward to a paradise regained.

Yea, truth and justice, then,
Will down return to men,
Orbed in a rainbow; and, like glories wearing,
Mercy will sit between,
Throned in celestial sheen,
With radiant feet the tissued clouds down steering;
And heaven, as at some festival,
Will open wide the gates of her high palace hall."

Then the remaining temples of idolatry will be consecrated to the worship of God, and the world will wonder at the stories of past ignorance and shame.

IV.

THE THIRD COMMANDMENT.

Honor to the Name of God.

THOU SHALT NOT TAKE THE NAME OF THE LORD THY GOD IN VAIN: FOR THE LORD WILL NOT HOLD HIM GUILTLESS THAT TAKETH HIS NAME IN VAIN.—Exodus xx, 7.

THE first commandment and the second require the worship of God alone; the third commandment also guards the character of God.

To "take the name of God" is to employ it in any way, by utterance, writing, or symbol. The Hebrew word rendered "in vain" means originally "for evil;" and the commandment means, "Thou shalt not use the name of Jehovah, thy God, for any evil purpose, for the Lord will not regard as pure any person who uses his name for an evil purpose." The Septuagint translates the word by an expression which means in Greek "in vain," and this meaning seems to have been carelessly and almost universally consented to in modern times, though it falls far short of the full meaning of the commandment.

Undoubtedly the chief thing forbidden in this commandment is a false oath, or swearing to a lie; but it also forbids the use of the name of

God to accomplish any evil end; and, lastly, more by implication than by direct statement, it forbids useless or light and thoughtless swearing.

It is remarkable that eight of the Ten Commandments are negative. Each of them *forbids* a certain course of action, implying that all action which is not forbidden, of the kind embraced in the commandment, is right, and ought to be practiced. For instance, "Thou shalt not worship any other gods," implies that we must regard God as the Divine One. "Thou shalt not make any graven image," implies again that we *should worship God* without an image.

So this commandment, the third, forbidding the use of the name of God for an *evil* purpose, implies that we may and ought to use it for a good purpose. God is willing to be worshiped, is willing to be thought about, and to be the object of conversation and investigation, and especially that his regard for right should be employed to benefit man.

There is no possible greater insult to the Creator of the heavens and earth than to employ the influence of his name for an evil end. He is holy, which means, he is absolutely free from any and all wrong. His throne is righteousness. He hates all sin. He will surely reward the righteous; he will surely punish the sinner. The influence, therefore, of his name should be always for good, never for evil.

Whoever uses the name of God to accomplish a wrong end, or so as to tend to the production of evil, violates this commandment, and will not by the great Judge be deemed guiltless.

The most obvious and palpable violation of this commandment is by taking a false oath, or by appealing to God for the truth of a falsehood. A man thus makes use of what credit he has as a religious man to sustain a lie.

An oath is the deliberate affirmation that a statement is true, or that a certain promise will be performed, with an understanding that the Divine One is invoked to punish the person if the statement is not true, or if the promise is not performed. Swearing to a known falsehood, or the intentional failure to keep a promise sworn to, is called perjury. This is, in some instances, regarded by the state as a crime, and is punished according to the legal enactments.

Some have maintained that all oaths are wrong, and are positively prohibited by Christianity. Others have maintained that all oaths are useless, and that they should, therefore, never be required, and never taken. To accommodate these classes it is allowed to them, both in Great Britain and the United States, to substitute a solemn affirmation for an oath, in all cases where an oath is required by law, with an understanding that the civil penalties for the violation of a judicial affirmation shall be the same as for the violation of an oath. The breaking of such a solemn affirmation, or proof of the known falsity of the thing affirmed, is perjury in the law.

Oaths were common among the Israelites, and were even required, under certain circumstances, by the divine law. A few instances of oaths related in the Bible will illustrate the practice.

First, there are instances of what may be called private or voluntary oaths, made from choice, deliberately, when not prescribed by any law. Thus Abraham, when he undertook to rescue Lot from his enemies, swore that he would not take any of the property of the parties that had seized upon Lot; and when, after he had succeeded, the king of Sodom wished that he should be repaid, "Abraham said to the king of Sodom, I have lifted up my hand unto the Lord, the most high God, that I will not take anything that is thine, lest thou shouldest say, I have made Abraham rich." Gen. xiv, 22, 23. Here Abraham voluntarily bound himself by an oath, and kept it. So Abimelech requested Abraham to swear by God that he would not deal falsely with him, nor with his son, "and Abraham said, I will swear." "They sware, both of them." Gen. xxi, 22–24. Abraham also required his eldest servant to swear unto him with reference to selecting a wife for Isaac, and he took the oath, and kept it. (Genesis xxiv, 2–9.) So Abimelech and Isaac, Jacob and Laban, bound each other by oaths. Jacob, on his death-bed, required his son Joseph to swear that he should be buried in his own tomb, away from Egypt; and Joseph swore, and kept his oath. So David sware to Saul that he would not destroy his family, and kept his oath. (1 Samuel xxiv, 21, 22.)

There are many more instances of these private oaths mentioned in the Old Testament, and they are never pronounced to be wrong. In every instance when an oath was taken, the person was considered as bound to fulfill its requirements.

The second class of oaths are civil oaths, or those taken according to the prescribed forms in judicial transactions. Thus witnesses under the Israelitish law were often put under oath, and if their testimony was false could be punished for perjury.

There can be no doubt that swearing became so common, so careless, among the Jews, as to excite the deepest indignation of the prophets. Therefore Jeremiah and Hosea both say, "Because of swearing the land mourneth."

There is, however, in the Old Testament nothing like a prohibition of an oath, whenever a person thought best to bring himself deliberately under its obligations. He might do it privately or publicly; but he was required to do it, if at all, deliberately and solemnly, and to hold himself bound by his oath. Indeed, both Isaiah and Jeremiah say, "He that sweareth in the earth shall swear by the God of truth." Isaiah lxv, 16; Jeremiah xii, 16.

It is evident that in the time of Christ the taking of oaths had become so common, and was resorted to on such trivial occasions, that the sacredness of the practice was overlooked. It was also common to pretend to avoid the sacredness of a genuine oath by using a senseless form of words, substituting for the name of God in the oath "the heavens," or "the life," or "the temple," or "the head," or some other precious object. This was a foolish practice, as common now as it was then. Jesus rebuked it as both useless and wrong. He said in his great sermon on the Mount: "Ye have heard that it hath been said by them of old time, Thou shalt not forswear thyself, but shalt perform unto the Lord thine oaths: but I say unto you, Swear not at all." Now did Jesus mean that a man should never swear by the right object, that is, in the name of God himself? The context seems to determine the question. He does not disapprove of what the Old Testament requires, but only adds to it. It was as much as to say, "The old law requires that you should not swear *falsely;* that is all right, and as much as men could bear and understand then, but I have something more to add: "SWEAR NOT AT ALL." And in order that this might not be misunderstood, he explains what he means thus: "Neither by heaven"—observe that he does not say, "Swear not, even by God," for that had been allowed and commanded—but "neither by *heaven*, for it is God's throne;" that is, heaven is entirely out of your control, and it is simply foolish for you to swear by it; "nor by the earth, for it is his footstool," you cannot control the earth; "neither by Jerusalem, for it is the city of the great King;" it is not your city, and you cannot control it: "neither shalt thou swear by thy head, because thou canst not make one hair white or black. But let your communication be, Yea, yea: nay, nay: for whatsoever is more than these cometh of evil."

This is a most pointed prohibition of common conversational swearing by indiscriminate and miscellaneous objects. It seems to imply that if any oath is allowed it should be, according to the old law, deliberate, and confined to a reference to the will of the great God, with whom alone we are connected, to confirm our truthfulness hereafter by his rewards and punishments.

The Apostle James afterward, when exhorting Christians not to be impatient under their sufferings, says: "Above all things, my brethren, swear not, neither by heaven, neither by earth, neither by any other oath; but let your yea be yea, and your nay, nay; lest ye fall into condemnation." The swearing here forbidden is that to which men when maltreated would feel inclined. It was not judicial or deliberate oaths.

In the New Testament oaths are alluded to as justifiable and proper. In the Epistle to the Hebrews we read: "For when God made promise to Abraham, because he could swear by no greater, he sware by himself." "Wherein God, willing more abundantly to show unto the heirs of promise the immutability of his counsel, confirmed it with an oath." Jesus Christ himself also, just before his crucifixion, seems to me to have taken a solemn judicial oath, swearing to his own Messiahship. He was on trial, and to all their questions made no answer till the high priest put him under oath with these words: "I adjure thee by the living God"—that is, I put thee under a solemn oath by the living God—"that thou tell us whether thou be the Christ, the Son of God." Then, and not till then, we have his answer; nor did he object to the oath.

It is easy to fall into the extreme of superstition, and that seems to be a superstitious feeling which pronounces it wrong to do what not only the patriarchs and prophets, but also the disciples of Christ, and the great Teacher himself, did. As the apostle well says, "For men verily swear by a greater, and an oath for confirmation is an end of all strife." So, if men are truthful and religious, it will always be. An oath therefore is right if it is taken deliberately and conscientiously, and strictly adhered to.

Some who acknowledge the *rightfulness* of oaths, maintain that among good men they are *unnecessary*, and are even apt to become pernicious. They are unnecessary, it is urged, because a good man's word should be as true and binding as an oath. They are pernicious, it is said, because the use of them tends to depreciate a mere statement without an oath. Men reason thus: If an oath is necessary to make a promise binding, of course without an oath it is excusable to lie. Again, the frequent taking of oaths tends to lower respect for them, and there is undoubtedly, therefore, in all civilized countries much false swearing, and much demoralization of the public conscience.

All these objections have some force, but apply more to an abuse than to a right use of oaths. But, without a protracted discussion of these questions, I will present simply what appears to me the right conclusion. Oaths are required too frequently. Whenever administered it should be solemnly, and with a full understanding of their import. The practice of hurrying and slurring them over, muttering them in a tone of voice scarcely articulate, as is too common in our court-rooms and legislative halls, is very reprehensible.

False swearing is religiously a great crime, in heinousness and depth of impiety yielding only to deliberate blasphemy, which the Saviour seemed in particular instances to pronounce unpardonable. A perjurer, unrepenting and unreformed, should be deemed unworthy of any confidence or any intimacy. Society, for its own protection, should severely punish such a crime.

A man who would deliberately swear to support the Constitution of the United States, as all our public officers do, and then plot for its overthrow, deserves universal execration; and deserves, if any one does, confinement in a state prison. There is little hope for a people that can honor, or even tolerate, such men. That people which will tolerate false swearing are not far from ruin.

This commandment is also violated by light and thoughtless, and by hasty and passionate profanity. The common profanity of many persons is a great moral wrong. It is often reproved from the sacred desk; it is regarded by all religious denominations as an open violation of Christian covenant; it is by many Protestant denominations treated as a sufficient cause for exclusion from Church-fellowship; it is pronounced to be ungentlemanlike, and a violation of the requirements of good society; it would be regarded by all, even by those who practice it, as indicative of deep depravity and degradation in a woman, and yet in spite of all this it is heard often in the street, in public conveyances, and where men miscellaneously congregate.

How can we account for this? Some preachers, more earnest than philosophical, have attributed it entirely to depravity. This is a very summary way of disposing of the matter, but not very thorough. It betrays a want of acquaintance with men. A disease is half cured if you certainly know the cause. It is simply foolish to attribute what is commonly called swearing—though much of it is not swearing, not being in the form of an oath—to *depravity* alone. Many of these men whose conversation is interlarded with appellations of the Divine Being, and with words pertaining to the eternal condition of men, do not deliberately intend to *sin*, nor do they choose these words simply because they are wrong, and offensive to good men, and are by many regarded as indecent and ungentlemanly, but from some other reason. And it is likely if the intelligent among them—for a small minority among them are intelligent—should clearly perceive the cause, they would be able to apply the remedy.

The cause of common swearing is this. Under the influence of strong emotion it is natural for every person to use the most forcible expressions that he can command. It is not *thought* that he intends to express so much as *feeling*. Interjections, unmeaning exclamations, like the bleating of sheep and the barking of dogs, are natural. The most forcible words ever employed are those pertaining to death and eternity, to God and the devil. Therefore unthinking men in passion resort to these words. Every man of observation knows that, as a general truth, the most ignorant and uncultivated of wicked men are the most addicted to profanity. They use it in strong passion, and it soon becomes a fixed habit with them to use it on all occasions. Occasionally among unthinking men some may be found, especially where they are entirely excluded from good female society, who either swear, or use some strong expression connected with heaven or hell, in every sentence. It seems almost a pity to deprive such men of this privilege, as really they are incapable of constructing a simple sentence without such an expression. If they find themselves in society where even they deem it disgraceful to swear, they generally have nothing to say. It is pure stupidity, and the consequent paucity of words, that leads them to profanity. A man who really has a variety of thought, and a good vocabulary of conversational terms, has never the necessity, and seldom a strong temptation, to this kind of speech. A good education is perhaps the best remedy for this habit. It is most common among men who either cannot or do not read or write.

Common light profanity is a great sin and a great disgrace. It hardens the heart and benumbs the conscience. It destroys even a correct taste. This applies to very much that is not directly included in the third commandment. To use the name of the devil or to speak of damnation is no dishonor to God; but all such expressions, employed either flippantly or in passion, betray a coarseness of feeling and a tendency to trifle with solemn things, and also prepare the way for actual false or vain swearing.

Perhaps some preachers of the Gospel themselves have contributed not a little to this tendency, by the unnecessary introduction of appellations of the Divine One in their sermons; and many pray in public as though they were talking *about* God rather than *to* him, and most ungrammatically as well as unnecessarily repeat his names, seemingly because they love to hear the sound. Why should educated ministers violate one of the fundamental rules of syntax and address God in the third person?

It is the characteristic of a highly cultivated

and devout man to cherish a profound reverence for God. It is said of an eminent scholar and divine, that he never mentioned the name of God without lifting his hat from his head. If this might be deemed eccentric, and certainly if it was done in an ostentatious way, it would be Pharisaical; yet how much more becoming does it seem than that reckless abuse of the name of God which characterizes the coarse and thoughtless, who seem to be utterly destitute of those highest and most honorable emotions of the human soul. We live in a country where forms are too little regarded for our own highest enjoyment and development.

But this commandment is most glaringly violated by appealing to the authority of God, or to the sanctions of religion, for the sustentation or success of a bad cause. How forcible the exclamation of Madame Roland when led off to the guillotine, "O liberty, what crimes have been perpetrated in thy name!" Well may we also reverently exclaim, O religion, what crimes have been perpetrated in thy name! It was to promote the cause of God that the millions of Europe poured down in successive avalanches upon Asia in the crusades, mercilessly overwhelming the unoffending populations, until by the true will of God they were wasted and scattered and destroyed! Every tyrant and despot claims to reign and to execute all his cruel and lustful purposes "by the grace of God!" The French Revolution, in its awful unreined revelry of carnage, into which it degenerated when its leaders became infuriated and lost their reason, was, nevertheless, honest enough not to pretend to act according to the direction of God. It stands almost alone in this regard among all the stupendous organized cruelties of man. Persecution, undertaken with the professed purpose of defending God and his cause, has slain actually in Europe alone many millions of men and women and children, and inflicted a reproach upon the honor of Christianity, which not without centuries of patient purity can be washed away. These acts of nations have been crimes of some individual men. Nations have no responsibility but through their men.

Now all this is a direct violation of this third commandment of the Decalogue. It is using the name and authority of God for an evil purpose. "Woe unto them that call evil good and good evil; that put darkness for light and light for darkness; that put bitter for sweet and sweet for bitter." These men who attribute to God the works of evil, or assume to invoke his blessing upon what they know, or ought to know, to be sin, violate this commandment far more grossly than their far less guilty and profane friends who utter profanity in every breath.

Thus, by adhering closely to the literal truth of this brief commandment, there is opened up to us an avenue of thought that seems interminable, both backward through the past and forward far down in the future. The more we study this Decalogue, the more will it seem worthy to have been engraved on stone by the finger of God. The first commandment. forbids man to recognize any power, fancied or real, as worthy of his homage, but the great God of the universe. How much of evil this, if obeyed, would sweep away; how much of good, if obeyed, would it accomplish!

The second commandment forbids all idolatry, which once enslaved the whole world, and has destroyed whole races of men by the vice it has engendered, and still holds half the world in slavish chains.

The third commandment forbids all irreverence for the name, and for whatever is connected with the name, of Jehovah. Whoever obeys it is thereby made a man! Reverence for God becomes a pole-star to guide him ever into higher life. Men imitate whom they revere.

Properly carried out it would lead to a high respect to whatever is historically, or by man's actions, peculiarly associated with the presence or power or goodness of God.

V.

THE FOURTH COMMANDMENT.

The Holy Sabbath.

REMEMBER THE SABBATH DAY, TO KEEP IT HOLY. SIX DAYS SHALT THOU LABOR, AND DO ALL THY WORK: BUT THE SEVENTH DAY IS THE SABBATH OF THE LORD THY GOD: IN IT THOU SHALT NOT DO ANY WORK, THOU, NOR THY SON, NOR THY DAUGHTER, THY MANSERVANT, NOR THY MAIDSERVANT, NOR THY CATTLE, NOR THY STRANGER THAT IS WITHIN THY GATES. FOR IN SIX DAYS THE LORD MADE HEAVEN AND EARTH, THE SEA, AND ALL THAT IN THEM IS, AND RESTED THE SEVENTH DAY: WHEREFORE THE LORD BLESSED THE SABBATH DAY, AND HALLOWED IT. Exodus xx, 8–11.

IT is a phenomenon that must strike every observer as worthy of his careful attention, that many millions of the human race, embracing all complexions and several races, and spread over a large portion of the habitable globe, are accustomed to make every seventh day an exception to all the other days of the year, and devote themselves on that day to rest from labor, and recreation, or religious worship. Any other habit so general would be attributed to some physiological peculiarity, to some law of the body or the mind, or to some agency in the atmosphere or earth exerting a power on the conduct of men.

But we seek in vain for any natural cause of this appearance. It can be attributed only to this fountain head, the commandment received from Sinai by the Israelites more than four thousand years ago. Is there any other practical fact that so astonishingly exhibits the power of the Bible upon the character and conduct of men?

The commandment on the Sabbath is the most specific and the most minute in its directions of all the ten. It is not contented with the general requisition that the Sabbath day should be "holy." It also requires that all labor should be confined to the other six days of the week, and that no member of the family should be allowed to labor, and that no beast of burden or of service should be compelled to work for man, on the Sabbath.

A reason for the commandment is also given: to wit, "For in six days the Lord made heaven and earth, the sea, and all that in them is, and rested the seventh day: wherefore the Lord blessed the Sabbath day, and hallowed it."

Now our belief is that the whole of the Decalogue is binding upon all men, and that, in the words of Christ, "The Sabbath was made for MAN;" not for the Hebrews, but for all men.

WHAT IS THE SABBATH? Simply one day in seven, taken in regular order as it recurs, and devoted to religious culture.

Had the Sabbath been regularly observed

from the creation of man to the present time, it would now recur, of course, on a day from which, counting backward by sevens, we should arrive at the first rest-day of God after the creation of man.

The Jews claim that their Sabbath, our Saturday, is that day. This claim is generally acknowledged by Christians, though there are some who maintain that it can be chronologically demonstrated that, on account of some confusion, in time of disaster and revolution and ignorance, the Jews are themselves mistaken, and that the genuine Sabbath is our Sunday, wrongly called "the first day of the week."

There is no good reason, however, for denying that the Jewish Sabbath is the true seventh day, reckoning from the creation of man, and that the Christian Sunday is the first day of the Hebrew week, or of the genuine week.

A change so great as transferring the Sabbath from the seventh to the first day of the week could not be made but by divine authority. If a society of men, a Church, or a denomination, could change the Sabbath from the last day of the week to the first, then another society, Church, or denomination could change it to the second day, or to any other day, and the result would be a number of Sabbaths, conflicting with each other, and thus destroying one of its grand objects, order and harmony.

If the Sabbath, therefore, was ever changed, it must have been done by Christ or his apostles.

Such was the fact.

The change does not seem to have been brought about by a sudden edict, but by a quiet, persistent urging of a new custom. The apostles and early Christians seem to have been in the habit of meeting together for religious services on Sunday, or the first day of the week, and soon they began to claim that to observe the seventh day, or the Sabbath-day as it was called, in addition to the first day, was not binding upon them. Thus we read in the history of the Apostles, "And upon the first day of the week, when the disciples came together to break bread, Paul preached unto them, ready to depart on the morrow." Acts xx, 7. Again: "Upon the first day of the week, let every one of you lay by him in store, as God hath prospered him." 1 Cor. xvi, 2. But with regard to the last day of the week we read: "Let no man, therefore, judge you in meat, or in drink, or in respect of an holy day, or of the new moon, *or of the Sabbath days*." Col. ii, 16. All these things Christians were to discard, or from the strict laws about them they were absolved.

It follows, then, that either Christ and his apostles assumed to nullify one of the Ten Commandments, or they substituted the first day of the week as the Sabbath for the last day of the week, previously observed.

Now that Christ and his apostles assumed to nullify a commandment in the Decalogue no man of sound judgment could believe. Repeatedly Christ acknowledged and asserted the divine authority of the Decalogue. To repeal it would have been to set himself in direct contradiction to what he pronounced the law of God. Such a repeal, if conceivable, must have been open, direct, and formal, or it would not be believed.

The facts seem to be, that the Sabbath is an institution founded upon man's nature and God's will, and therefore *absolutely irrepealable.* The decision of the date of the Sabbath, whether on the first day or the seventh day of the week, must be made by divine authority. Either, so far as man can see, would be proper; neither is preferable to the other. The seventh day was the one first chosen, but if it was made known to all mankind, all had lost it except the Jews; and when the Gospel by Christ was to be preached, it was found more practicable to secure an observance of the first day of the week as a truly holy day, than to emancipate the seventh day of the week from its false associations. Moreover, the first day of the week was the day on which Christ arose from the dead, demonstrating man's immortality. Therefore

Christians were taught to regard the first day as their Sabbath; and inasmuch as Christians are destined to cover the earth and control it, the first day of the week is to become the universal Sabbath.

But this change of time does not affect the *true* character of the Sabbath. It does make it easier to discard all the false restrictions and associations begotten by the traditions of the Jewish teachers, and carries the Sabbath back to the purity of the Decalogue, which coincides with the pure light of Christ and his apostles.

HOW, THEN, IS THE SABBATH TO BE OBSERVED?

There is to be a cessation of all labor put forth to secure our own gratification or reward.

Labor necessary to execute other commands of God, and impulses of a holy nature, is allowed—such as to feed the hungry, to protect and comfort and heal the sick, even to rescue animals from suffering, to save property from unexpected destruction by fire or water.

"The Sabbath was made for man, and not man for the Sabbath." The Sabbath should be accepted as a blessing, not submitted to as a burden. It is not designed to deprive a man of any real good, but to favor him with rest, and time for religious worship.

To suppose that it is wrong on the Sabbath to do any work needful for the relief of suffering is superstitious. To suppose that God intended to make the Sabbath an evil, by depriving men on that day of what would really promote their physical, mental, and moral good, is completely to misunderstand the purpose of God, and, like the Pharisees of old, to convert a blessing into a curse.

To understand how properly to keep the Sabbath, one must reflect upon its object. Whatever course of conduct tends to secure its object is right; all other conduct is wrong.

Its object is man's rest; that he may be benefitted bodily, mentally, spiritually, and that God may be thus honored.

Man is to rest from labor for his own good. A periodical cessation from labor, it has been found, is conducive to man's highest development and soundest health.

Is he a farmer? He should on the Sabbath rest from all labor of body or mind connected with the management of his farm. He should do nothing directly for profit. What is needful to secure his property from destruction, or to save man or beast from suffering, he should do.

The Sabbath was not designed directly or indirectly to produce suffering, or the waste of property. It is a blessing, not a curse.

Is the man a student? Is it his business to read or write or investigate science or truth? On the Sabbath he should rest from that toil.

The farmer may study on the Sabbath, and thereby, perhaps, rest; but the student by so doing is directly violating the spirit of the Sabbath.

The Sabbath should be devoted primarily to spiritual culture. It has been so employed from time immemorial. It is the day of holy convocation; for the public hearing of the Bible and authorized explanations of it, and the public worship of God.

No element of civilization is more patent than this. Without this Christianity fails and the human race perishes. The grand hope of humanity is centered in the Sabbath.

Let it not be asserted that were there no Sabbath men would be just as devout, and religious gatherings would be just as frequent, and the principles of morality and religion just as faithfully taught. Facts do not justify such an assertion. Reason does not sanction it. The wisdom of God is exhibited by the successful results that always flow from a proper observance of the Sabbath.

Many questions of interest arise connected with this subject.

Politically, it may be asked, Should the observance of the Sabbath be required by civil law?

This opens up for investigation the general subject, the proper object of civil law. The profoundest Christian statesmen and moralists are coming clearly to see that in moral teaching the Church should lead and the state follow. The object of the state is, not to require religion or morality by force, but to protect life, liberty, and property. If the state enacts a law for the observance of the Sabbath, it is to secure the political good of the people. This law is not designed to reach a religious result, but a benefit that shall be enjoyed by all, whether religious or not.

Such a law is proper and should be enforced. But no man keeps the Sabbath in a manner acceptable to God, who is deterred from its open violation only by the fear of the law.

Should work that cannot well cease at the close of six days be entered upon by Christians?

We answer, It is the will of God that all should be Christians, and if such work is proper for any, it is for them. Can any doubt that long sea voyages are proper, even though the ship must be attended to on the Sabbath? The reducing of metals from the ore, the evaporation of water from salt, and many other kinds of labor, often require several weeks of steady work, without any regular intermission on the seventh day.

In such cases intelligent, cultivated Christians will observe the spirit, while compelled to violate the letter, of the law. They will sacredly devote one seventh of the time to rest and religious culture. They will make this time as far as possible correspond with the true Sabbath. An honest effort to do so will remove nearly all of the practical difficulty. If a portion or all of the Sabbath must be devoted to labor, an equal amount of time will be properly consecrated to rest and religion at the first opportunity.

The rest from labor provided for by the Sabbath is absolutely necessary to prevent disease, insanity, and premature death. A proper observance of the Sabbath would probably diminish the instances of disease, and particularly of insanity, more than half.

THE BENEFITS OF THE SABBATH cannot be overstated.

Whether the heart, head, or lungs are most essential to the life, who can decide? Whether the Bible, the Church, or the Sabbath is the most essential to Christianity, it is idle to inquire. Christianity rests upon the Sabbath. The enemies of Christianity instinctively attack the Sabbath.

The Sabbath was appointed by God. Its origin cannot otherwise be accounted for. There is no clear foundation in nature for the division of time into weeks of seven days; but we are told that after six days, or periods of labor, God rested on the seventh day.

Let this not be lightly passed over as the fancy of an undeveloped mind. God himself may have his times of exertion and of rest. The days of creation were "days of the Lord," not days of man, and "with the Lord one day is as a thousand years, and a thouand years as one day." The first Sabbath of Jehovah since the creation of the world may not yet have passed. What shall be developed when God's days of labor recommence, who shall imagine? We are to imitate God in labor and in rest, and this fact, revealed to us in the Decalogue, is a sufficient reason for this commandment.

Facts prove it to be beneficial.

The Sabbath screens those who observe it from idleness on the one hand and from excessive labor on the other. "Six days shalt thou work" is one part of the commandment; "Remember the Sabbath-day to keep it holy" is the other. Idleness is ruin. Excessive labor destroys life. The hebdomadal division of time is found by experience to be right.

Six hundred and forty-one physicians signed a petition to the British Parliament against opening the Crystal Palace on Sundays, in which they said: "Your petitioners, from their acquaintance with the laboring classes, and with the laws that regulate the human economy, are convinced that a seventh day of rest, instituted by God, and coeval with the existence of man, is essential to the bodily health of man in every station of life."

The experiment of observing and of breaking the Sabbath has been tried frequently by large bodies of men, always proving the practical advantages of observing a seventh day of rest.

The Sabbath is a great safeguard against barbarism. Its effect upon the cleanliness, the good appearance, and the culture of a people who observe, it cannot be over-estimated.

Can a better view of a perfect world be imagined than a Sabbath-keeping world? Behold the picture as it shall yet be seen by angels and men.

The shades of night slowly roll away before the dawn of day. As the darkness thus retires before the sun, the people in the country, in the village, and in the city, rising from their night's repose, all worship God. As the day advances the ringing bells announce the time of public worship, and without exception all assemble in their churches for the public worship of God. Can crime, disorder, poverty, exist among such a people? Would not the earth be an ante-chamber of heaven, did all the world observe the Sabbath?

That glorious sight shall yet be seen. To bring it about we must rely principally upon moral power. The nature, sanctions, privileges, and beauties of the Sabbath must be made known: its boon to the poor man, its benefit to the rich, its barrier against oppression and degradation, its promotion of order and general prosperity. It is an ordinance of God; observed with the right motives, it will secure prosperity to an individual, a family, a nation: broken, it is the sure precursor of ruin.

VI.

THE FIFTH COMMANDMENT.

Duty toward Parents.

HONOR THY FATHER AND THY MOTHER: THAT THY DAYS MAY BE LONG UPON THE LAND WHICH THE LORD THY GOD GIVETH THEE.—Exodus xx, 12.

THIS is the first positive commandment in the Decalogue. The preceding four forbid, and by implication require; this requires, and by implication forbids.

There is no commandment in the Decalogue requiring parents to protect and love their children, though this requires children to honor their parents. The reason of this distinction is, probably, that God has implanted in the parent, and particularly in the mother, an *instinct* which prompts them to love their children, an instinct strong so soon as it is able to act, and which tends to ripen into a reasonable affection. This instinct is not peculiar to human beings.

Instinct is indeed a wonderful power. Without knowledge, it commands all resources necessary to success; without reason, it has all the wisdom requisite to attain its ends. The young birds that have never been trained by parental care, hatched from the eggs by artificial heat, and kept carefully separated from all birds of their own species or others, will, when the parental instinct prompts them to it, construct a nest for their eggs of just the material used, and just according to the plan pursued, from the beginning, by birds of their kind. The beaver fells trees, and builds his dam across the stream according to the highest skill of engineering science. The solitary wasp bores a hole in the ground, deposits the eggs at the bottom, and then seeks some grubs, and fills the hole with just enough to supply her offspring with food till able to take care of themselves.

Instinct is that power which impels animals, including man, to secure the welfare of themselves as individuals, and of their species, and also to subserve other wise purposes, without evidence of an understanding, on their part, of the wisdom of the course which they pursue. They do not reach a knowledge of the excellence of their course by study by an examination of different plans, by experiment accompanied with frequent failures; but at once, and spontaneously. This power of instinct is undoubtedly a direct exhibition of the wisdom of God through them, acting without individual consciousness and reason. And yet this instinct, even in brutes, is capable of being slightly modified by their own reason. It can also be changed by cultivation. Its chief characteristic is, that it is evidently intended for the present good of the individual and his kind.

Man, being endowed with the higher powers of reason, has less instinct than any other animal; indeed he has only so much as is absolutely necessary for the preservation of the species, which could not be secured by reason alone.

Among these few instincts is the spontaneous, unreasoning love of the mother for the child. This attachment soon ripens into strong, probably the strongest of all love; a love which often defies all obstacles, physical and moral, and is not shut off by the grave. What is so tender, so all-embracing and eternal, as a mother's love? The father, too, where God's own institution of the family is properly observed, shares in this attachment to their child, so that, by the common sentiment of all cultivated men, the parents who do not protect and exhibit affection for their children are regarded as monsters, deserving the severe disapprobation of all. It was for this reason that it was deemed unnecessary to incorporate into the Decalogue a commandment for parents to love and protect their children.

But children are not *instinctively* taught to love and honor their parents. These feelings on the part of the child are of slow growth. They are responsive to the affection of the mother and the attention of the father. They reward the parents for their solicitude and labor. They may be cultivated or repressed.

But it is not primarily or principally to *children* that this commandment is directed. Children naturally, if not instinctively, do honor their parents. If not, it is almost invariably the fault of the parents themselves, who, either by improvidence, or heartlessness, or caprice, or cruelty, have repelled the affections of their children. This commandment is addressed to *older persons;* to youth, and to men and women. Long as parents live they should be honored; and the more, if possible, the older they become.

So far as the attachment of parents to their children is only instinctive it soon disappears. Instinct, which is a substitute for reason, is much stronger in brutes than in men; and its peculiar character is seen particularly in this instance, inasmuch as it unites parents and offspring among animals only so long as the union is necessary for the preservation of life. The mother animal repels her young so soon as they can take care of themselves, and in turn is treated as a stranger by the offspring. The attachment is made to vary, by the Author of the instinct, with the demand.

In some animals it lasts, perhaps, a year; in others but a few hours; while the ostrich, laying her eggs on the hot sand of the desert, never seeks her young, which are hatched by the sun, and grow up and learn to run and fly without parental watchcare or instruction.

Man, though an animal, is also an immortal and responsible being. His instincts, the possession of which shows his animal nature, are scanty and short-lived; reason, which evinces his immortal nature, enters to sit upon the throne of the soul. Therefore, when instinct ceases to act, reason requires that the mother and father should contiuue to protect and instruct their child; and when even the child reaches manhood, they should still have a peculiar regard and affection for him. This, though not required in the Decalogue, is elsewhere taught in the Bible.

Precisely so, that attachment to the mother and father which the child feels, is at first nothing but an unreasoning, selfish gratitude for favors received, encouraged, perhaps, by the feeling that more favors of the same kind can be obtained at pleasure. The child exhibits a feebler love for the parent's strong love. While the dependence exists, what is there praiseworthy in that? Its absence would, indeed, mark the child as a monster; its presence, however, is so natural, and may be conjoined with such unworthiness in other respects, that it is never alone regarded as worthy of particular credit.

But the honor to father and mother that continues after the parents can do nothing more to bless their child, the regard shown to them when the son and daughter have reached such a stage of development that they justly feel that they must now rely on their own judgment, this it is not unfrequently difficult to render; this it is that forms the burden of the fifth commandment.

Now it is presumable that there must be some profound reasons in the nature of things for the incorporation of this precept into the comprehensive Decalogue. A careful and candid examination will show the truth of this presumption. This commandment is worthy of its place because it particularly recognizes and renders sacred the family relation. It assumes that the father and mother, who are to be honored by their children as long as they live, are united together for life by the indissoluble compact of marriage. Otherwise they could not be jointly and equally honored.

Perhaps the most painful and touching testimony upon the enormous iniquity of slavery was given indirectly by a Northern clergyman, who visited the South and wrote a strong and labored defense of slavery, in the course of which he confesses that he felt an inexpressible sympathy for a company of slave-children that he undertook to address in a religious meeting, from the conviction that he could not make them fully comprehend the meaning of the first words in the Lord's Prayer: "OUR FATHER which art in heaven!" What idea could these slave-children have of a *human* father? How could they honor him? Many knew not who their fathers were. If their fathers were slaves they had no control over them, did not provide for them, and did not seem worthy of their honor or love. Even their mothers had no power to instruct and govern them, still less their fathers! How, then, could the poor slave-children honor their human father and mother? How could they comprehend, then, the touching appellation of the Divine Being, "OUR FATHER," founded on the experience of the regard and love of a human father? Similar must be the condition of all who cannot honor their father and mother. They cannot understand the very beginning of the Lord's Prayer.

This commandment presupposes not only the sacredness of the marriage relation, binding father and mother together for life, but also that high development of industry, economy, providence, mutual forbearance, and affection which unite the members of a family together.

Now the family relation is the source of all order, of all government, of all industry, of all peace, of all the thorough and permanent and harmonious development among men. Whatever strikes a blow at this relation strikes at the very heart of humanity. It matters not with what intent it is aimed, what high-sounding sophistry may defend it, what delusive dreams may tempt to it, or what passion may demand it; the result must be to degrade and bestialize and destroy. The family circle is the monad out of which the whole fabric of true society grows. It is the prime cellule in which the organic life commences. The patriarchal government is the oldest of governments, and all others truly valuable are developed out of that. As a simple air like "Auld Lang Syne" can by a skillful musician be presented in many variations, some in harmony rich and complicated, yet all preserving the original melody, and good in proportion to the preservation of the fundamental tune, so out of a good family government may be developed pure democracy, aristocracy, monarchy, representative republicanism; but none can accomplish their purpose unless the original family government is maintained.

A state made up of well-regulated families, though its constitution were the most faulty imaginable, would be well managed; but if the families were not on the average orderly, though the theory of its political government were perfect, it would be little better than an anarchy.

This is the philosophy of that wonderful promise attached to this commandment. Honor thy father and thy mother, *that thy days may be long in the land which the Lord thy God giveth thee.* This is not the promise of a long life *individually* to the child that honors his parents. Many children honor their parents and die young. I do not deny that honoring father and mother has a tendency to lengthen the life of an individual child, both naturally and by the blessing of God. All virtue tends toward long life. But the chief burden of the promise is, *long life to a nation* in which the children generally honor their parents. This is evident from the peculiar phraseology, "in the land which the Lord thy God giveth thee." God gave the Israelites primarily a land. So long as they were a nation they should keep that land. The length of their days in that land, that is, the length of time in which they should be a thriving nation, unconquered and independent, should depend upon their obedience to this commandment, "Honor thy father and thy mother."

God works by general principles. Other nations have their lands assigned them. "God hath made of one blood all natious of men for to dwell on all the face of the earth, and hath appointed unto them their habitations." He has given to the mingled Goths and Celts and Africans this land in North America, and the length of time we and our descendants shall abide here a flourishing people, will depend largely upon our obedience to this commandment, "Honor thy father and thy mother."

I believe that a careful study of the institutions of man, and especially of nations, will prove beyond the possibility of denial, that no people who have been in the habit of honoring father and mother have ever degenerated or been subdued so as to be lost; and that no nation which has loosened the holy restraints of the family circle—which is more effectually done by disobedience to this command than in any other way—have ever been for a long time vigorous and growing.

The oldest nation on the face of the earth, and embracing nearly a fourth of all the population in the world, are more remarkable for this trait than for any other: children honor their parents there till they die, and even perpetuate a grateful religious remembrance of them after death. On this subject I cannot express my convictions better than by quoting from a work lately published, entitled "Life among the Chinese," by a missionary who had spent thirteen years in one of the largest cities of that nation:

"It is a noteworthy fact, that of all those ancient empires founded immediately subsequent to the deluge, China alone remains. The Assyrians, Egyptians, and, in later times, the Grecians, have severally attained to a comparatively high degree of intelligence and refinement; but their star soon culminated and sank into utter darkness. China, however, has never been wrecked, her civilization has never retrograded; paradoxical though it seems, her star has remained in its zenith for at least three thousand years. Through all this long lapse of centuries the Chinese have kept up fairly and steadily to their original civilization; and to-day they present all the essential elements of those social, literary, and political traits which characterized them in those early epochs when the Assyrians built their magnificent cities, the Egyptians developed the subtle theory of the metempsychosis, or the Greeks were thundering at the gates of Troy. It must certainly be interesting to inquire how such a result has been reached, and to ascertain, if we can, at least some of the causes which have contributed to it. In solving this interesting problem we observe that the civilization of the Chinese is distinguished from all other heathen civilizations by the fact that its primitive elements were derived from the Bible, and that the necessary tendency of these elements is to conserve and perpetuate the system. A prominent characteristic of Chinese civilization is the total absence of those revolting and cruel rites which form the leading treats of other heathen systems of civilization. As illustrative of this remark, we may refer to the deification of vice and the offering of human victims in sacrifices, practices which, though characteristic of nearly every other heathen nation, constitute no feature of Chinese civilization. The connection between these abominations and the destruction of the nations guilty of them is shown in Leviticus xviii, 24, 25: 'Defile not ye yourselves in any of these things; for in all these the nations are defiled which I cast out before you; and the land is defiled: therefore I do visit the iniquity thereof upon it, and the land itself vomiteth out her inhabitants.' As a further contribution to the solution of this question we refer to the length of days promised by the Almighty to those who observed the command, 'Honor thy father and thy mother.' No heathen nation has ever approximated the Chinese in their respect for parents; and notwithstanding the wide divergence of the Chinese, both in theory and practice, from the true import of the fifth commandment, we conceive it is neither fanciful nor far-fetched to suppose that even their imperfect observance of it has had much to do with the permanence of their institutions and the perpetuity of their national existence." *

* Life among the Chinese: with Characteristic Sketches and Incidents of Missionary Operations and Prospects in China. By Rev. R. S. Maclay, M.A. New York: Carlton & Porter.

This view is undoubtedly correct. Indeed, on this account I deem it proper that all our public schools, supported by the state, should be required particularly to inculcate this virtue, which supports the foundation of the state—a proper regard to the authority and character of father and mother. Government is sapped at its very foundations if parental authority is defied. Happy is that nation whose parents generally deserve honor from their children and obtain it. Few are disorderly and criminal abroad who are taught to honor as well as love their parents at home.

Let us observe, then, the comprehensiveness of this commandment, descending to particulars.

1. It is comparatively easy to honor father and mother when they exhibit in all respects such a character as commands the honor of other men. If they are well-educated, and perhaps wealthy, and occupy respectable positions in society, it is natural that their children should be proud of them. But is this a fulfillment of the commandment? It is easy to appear to be virtuous when there is no temptation to vice; but is this virtue? Why should a rich man steal? Does he deserve credit because he does not rob a poor man of his only dollar?

This commandment is not fully obeyed in spirit unless it will bear the test of strong trial. A mother's love will cling to a prodigal son or daughter even when the world casts them off, and proudly go down into the purlieus of degradation to win the lost one back. Ought not the child's love to be like that? The father may be poor and ignorant; misfortune may have bowed him down and broken his spirits; ill health may have prostrated him, yes, even intemperance or crime may have overcome him. He himself in former years, (before he was so degraded,) or circumstances, or the affection of a mother, or a kind Providence, working you know not how, may have made you much superior to your father in moral stamina, in self-control, in dignity, in position, in the world's esteem: still honor him. Honor him as a father; for often it is given to a son to repay a father with a large compound interest for the small favors of protection and love in childhood. In many an instance virtue and piety on the part of son or daughter has won a parent's heart away from vice to integrity and religion.

Indeed, there is probably no feeling stronger in the heart of father and mother than a desire to be worthy of the love and honor of their children. Many a man, victim himself to some degrading habit, will plead earnestly with his children to abstain from the same practice, and will be nerved to extraordinary efforts to conquer himself for the sake of his children. In this way our Sabbath schools have had almost as much effect upon parents as upon children. Many a man has emancipated himself from the degrading habits of drunkenness, to secure the respect and the welfare of his children; and even should he not succeed, it would be the duty of the children to honor their father, even while they manfully withstood the evil influence of his example. In many instances the pleading of a prattling child has caused the drunken to reform.

If this is true in cases of real degradation, how impious is it for son or daughter to fail in respect for parents on account of their ignorance or poverty. Language has no terms too strong to express the indignation of a virtuous heart at such conduct. A man in the prime of life, in the presence of his little son, inflicted a great wrong upon his aged father, when he was astonished to hear from his little child, "That is the way, father, I will do to you when I am a man." The rebuke cut him to the heart, and led to immediate repentance.

Dramatists and novelists have resorted to the portrayal both of filial love and filial ingratitude to display their strongest power. Who has not heard of Æneas, the fabulous founder of the Roman people, who, permitted to carry away from the ruins of Troy as much treasure as his strength could bear, lifted upon his shoulders his aged and infirm father, Anchises, and won the admiration of both friends and foes? The great dramatist, Shakspeare, in one of his strongest tragedies, King Lear, has shown

> "How sharper than a serpent's tooth it is
> To have a thankless child."

Who that has read it has not had his soul moved to the deepest execration of the selfish wickedness of Goneril and Regan, and admiration of the devoted Cordelia? The dramatist knew how to touch the heart. Undoubtedly both classes of daughters are found in actual life. When Dickens was publishing in serial numbers several years ago his work, then entitled "The Old Curiosity Shop," in which he depicts with inimitable power that wonderful character, "Little Nellie," so remarkable for filial affection for her old wandering insane father, so intense was the interest awakened in that beautiful child, the creature of his fancy, that it is said he received letters from different parts of England and America, even from west of the Mississippi, begging him not to kill little Nell. But the demands of the story were inexorable, and little Nell died. And how touching is the elegy pronounced over the faithful child's grave! So, under the direction of the great Author of life's real dramas, how many faithful children meet no open reward for their fidelity in this life: no reward of applause; no reward in many or in length of years. But virtue always bears its own intrinsic fruit, the consciousness of rectitude and the blessings of eternal life. It seems unnatural for a child to honor a parent who has failed in duty toward him; yet as the child grows older, if won to virtue by the grace of God, he should bestow on his parents even unmerited love.

2. Again, it is comparatively easy for a child to honor his parents while he is a child, but it often becomes more and more difficult as the years advance. There comes a time in life when parental anxiety and the parental will begin to appear irksome and burdensome. The daughter wishes to declare her independence; the son regards the fears of the mother as indicative of a want of that confidence which he thinks is due to him, and the restraints of a father are felt to be something much like tyranny. Sometimes these feelings are not wholly without just cause, for unfortunately human fathers and mothers are not perfect; and some are overbearing and unsympathetic, and some are incapable of appreciating the passions and ambitions of their children, if unlike what they passed through, or if, as is often the case, they are destitute of a thorough recollection of what they themselves once were.

Then come some of the severest temptations of young people. They must to a certain extent decide for themselves. Every person has an independent will. A father's virtue will not save son or daughter. A mother's devotion, or want of it, will not fix the destiny of her child. The youth must write his own name on the debtor or creditor side of society. It must be entered by his own act among the good or evil. But even if he finds it necessary to assert his own manhood, to think his own thoughts, to shape his own principles, to take his own positions, can he not do it so as to honor father and mother? Can he not show that there is always a deep, abiding undercurrent of filial affection in his soul? That he always would, if possible, please father and mother? That to dissent from their wishes, even if duty calls him to it, is so far one of the most disagreeable actions of his life? If such be the character of a youth and a man, he will be prized and still more and more beloved by his parents, even though the particular anticipations which they have cherished be disappointed.

Wise parents never unnecessarily interfere with the choice of their children on matters which most concern them, and must affect chiefly their condition, further than to indicate the preference of the parents as one motive to be considered in the decision. And in no case is it necessary or proper to withhold that feeling which is required by the commandment, "Honor thy father and thy mother."

3. But of all kinds of disobedience to this commandment, clearly the most inexcusable and the worst are the instances in which the children of discreet, indulgent, and Christian parents forget their early instructions and abandon themselves to immorality and vice. Such instances, alas! too common, are alike mysterious to the philosopher, appalling to the moralist and the Christian, and the deepest of all possible afflictions to their parents. Mysterious and seemingly anomalous, because they appear to set at defiance the first principles of education, which impel philanthropic men to bring proper influences to bear upon young minds with an expectation of reward; but what encouragement can they have if the children of wise parents choose folly, and if those of religious parents plunge into sin? Appalling to Christians, for they seem directly to disprove and nullify a clear doctrine of the Bible, that if a child is properly trained he will not desert the right way. Indeed, so unnatural are such degenerate scions of a noble stock, that some theorists have assumed the position that all such persons necessarily prove that the parents, however wise and pious they my seem, must have been secretly faulty and vicious, or such unseemly results of their educa-

tion would not appear. The sentence is too sweeping, too uncharitable. Vice and virtue are closely akin. The strongest sweets make the strongest acids. "Great wit's to madness near allied." Every soul must choose for itself. Cain and Abel were sons of the same father and mother. No training, no counsel, no good example, no entreaty is omnipotent. Ofttimes the sweetest spices, the most beautiful flowers, grow from the rankest soil; while the plant carefully trained from the seed by the horticulturist bears an inferior flower or bitter fruit. If the chemistry of plants is uncontrollable, still more so are the mysterious laws of character and soul. Even the secrets of man's nature escape research. Its origin is the unseen mystery, the great insoluble enigma. It can finally be influenced only by moral motives, and by divine grace, and to be virtuous it must itself act. But it must never be forgotten, cannot be forgotten, that the worst of all men are those who, having had virtuous parents, choose vice. These are they who sin against the greatest light; they deliberately choose darkness because their deeds are evil. How often, when the child of pious parents is plunging into sin, must the thoughts of a father's disappointment and a mother's prayers smite the soul with desolation! What motive can reach a soul unmoved by that? And yet were the children of all pious parents pious, soon the world would be obedient to Christ.

4. The personal rewards of granting due honor to parents are great. One of the surest rewards of an earthly character is the reception of like honor from the generation that shall follow. There is no channel of influence in which the consequences of wrong and right action are more likely to show themselves. In an old and well-established society three generations are generally together. So, no doubt, under ordinary circumstances, it ought to be. If fathers and mothers do not honor their fathers and mothers, their children in like manner, when the time comes, will dishonor them. With some extraordinary exceptions, the rule of Christ will apply pre-eminently here: "In what measure ye mete it shall be measured to you again." Honor begets honor; neglect, neglect. The strongest talisman to throw around a son's or daughter's neck, to bind them to truth and to God, is the love of a virtuous home. This can be evinced in no other way so effectually as by cultivating the home virtues of respect for parents, love for children, and mutual fraternal regard.

Again; this alone furnishes a sufficiently high and noble object of life for the most of men and women. Few can govern states; few can sway multitudes with voice or pen; few can be great inventors or discoverers; few can control immense enterprises; and the most of those so favored find their scepter barren and life cheerless; but all can bless the family circle to which they belong. The first step toward it is to honor our parents; and this can be rightly done only by a true Christian life. When done, so comprehensive is its power, almost infallibly all other needed virtues follow in its train.

> "The sea of ambition is tempest tossed,
> And thy hopes may vanish like foam;
> But when sails are shivered and rudder lost,
> Then look for the light of home:
> And there, like a star through the midnight cloud,
> Thou shalt see the beacon bright;
> For never, till shining upon thy shroud,
> Can be quenched its holy light."

We conclude, then, with a deepened conviction that this commandment is worthy of a place in the Decalogue. Had those who first received it obeyed it, they would not now be a scattered people; but in the times of Christ they had specially made this commandment void by their vain traditions. Therefore they lost their territory and national life.

Here is a lesson for us. We are sadly degenerating in this respect. We are not equal to our Puritan fathers in our regard for parents and in our care over our children. The old Thanksgiving Festival, when two, three, or four generations used to gather together around the festal board, with the patriarch at the head, and the grandmother smilingly dispensing her benefits, looked up to with almost reverence by children and children's children, is not, I fear, so much prized now. Let us restore it in this new land, and especially observe the spirit of it during all the year. Happy are we if with the memories of home are connected the associations of home religion and family prayer. Happy if we can recall many such a scene as this:

> "Then kneeling down, to heaven's eternal King
>   The saint, the father, and the husband prays;
> Hope springs exultant on triumphant wing,
>   That thus they all shall meet in future days;
>   There ever bask in uncreated rays,
> No more to sigh, or shed the bitter tear,
>   Together hymning their Creator's praise,
> In such society, yet still more dear;
> While circling time moves round in an eternal sphere."

VII.

THE SIXTH COMMANDMENT.

The Sacredness of Human Life.

THOU SHALT NOT KILL.—Exodus xx, 13.

Two great and opposite mistakes may be made in the understanding of God's commandments. We may crowd into the language thought which it was not designed to express, and we may fail to draw out of the language all that it was really designed to express. Either, if intentional, is a criminal perversion of the Sacred Word.

Thus it would be reprehensible to maintain that the brief commandment, "Thou shalt not kill," is designed to forbid the killing of weeds, or trees, or insects, or animals of any kind. The occasion upon which the commandment was given, and the general tenor of the Scriptures, show such an interpretation would be unwarrantable and foolish. So, too, to maintain that this commandment absolutely forbids taking the life of a human being, *under any possible circumstances*, is inconsistent with the other teachings of God found in this same Bible, and also with certain primary instincts of our nature.

The other error, of emasculating the Bible, divesting it of its genuine meaning, and toning it down so as to correspond with our previously formed notions, is equally blamable, and far more common. There is a richness in biblical information and precept that cannot be appreciated without much study. How careful, therefore, ought the preacher to be, to find as nearly as possible the exact mind of the Spirit, the real intention of God in the language employed!

This has led me to study this comprehensive commandment, and I desire to aid you to come to a full and exact perception of the divine prohibition, "Thou shalt not kill."

1. It is evident that its scope must be confined to man. Over all other life, except human life, on this planet, man has supreme control. In this world God designed that man should be the tyrant, and all other living things his slaves. The patent-right to this nobility we find in the first charter of human authority, given to man by his Creator on the first day of man's existence, before as yet there had been a single Sabbath. "And God said, Let us make man in our own image, after our likeness; and let them," that is, let men, "have dominion over the fish of the sea, and over the fowl of the air, and over the cattle, and over all the earth, and over every creeping thing that creepeth on the earth."

It is not, therefore, cruel to pursue the whale even to the polar ocean, and plunge into his huge carcass the well-aimed harpoon; to draw from the water the finny tribes by the baited hook or the fatal net; to raise cattle for slaughter; to bring down birds by powder and shot; to destroy pernicious insects by the myriad, or to rob them of their silk or of their honey, or to crush them for their gorgeous colors to beautify our garments, or in any way to convert their properties to our gratification. They are our slaves, and we are their masters; and it is lawful for us to do what we will with our own. The patient ox may toil in our furrow and yield his flesh for our food; the cow and the goat may furnish us with milk and with meat, the sheep may clothe us with its abundant fleece, the camel may bear us over the tropical desert, and the reindeer over the polar snow, the intelligent dog may guard our property and be our companion, and everything that hath breath may justly be compelled to yield its treasures of muscle and mind for our convenience and pleasure, for we are their masters and they are our slaves.

It is probable, as an ingenious and well-informed writer has lately attempted to show, that man by an unwise and indiscriminate interference with vegetable and animal life has actually much injured the earth; but that does not disprove his right to do it wisely. Nor does this right justify cruelty to animals. The man who abuses his power, and inflicts needless pain on sentient creatures, who beats an inferior animal in passion, or for the devilish sport of seeing the signs of torture, who trains beasts to fight in his presence, or mercilessly slaughters brutes—such a man is a brute himself of the lowest order. He is like a terrier dog, or a hyena. He perverts his higher intelligence to abuse what God created for good. He deserves punishment, for the sake of suppressing evil example. The laws to prevent cruelty to animals are wise, and ought to be enforced.

Folly, too, in taking the life of the inferior animals ought to be rebuked. The practice of killing inoffensive birds and other animals, merely for the pleasure of seeing them die, or of cultivating skill in robbing them of life, is a hound-like gratification, not to be commended in a man except within narrow limits. And whenever it tends to destroy a proper balance of animal and vegetable life, or when it tends to allow the too great production of insects and vermin that these animals would consume, it ought to be condemned; and, if need be, the state may justly protect inoffensive and useful animals against the hunting propensity of men. But this protection, it should be observed, is founded on policy, not on right. It is never wicked to kill a bird, or a rabbit, or any other animal; it may be poor policy to do so. And if the life of an animal is protected by law, it should be only for the sake of some convenience or temporal advantage to man, and not because there is anything sacred in an animal's life. I do not deny, too, that the sportsman's pleasure is legitimate and proper. I believe it is a part of human nature that we may justly indulge to a certain extent. It is to those who cultivate it healthful and invigorating, provided that it be tempered with discretion. The life of animals is justly in the power of man.

But when we reach *human life* we pass over to entirely another sphere of God's works. The difference between an ape and a man is greater than between earth and heaven. There is no gradually ascending scale by which you can mount from an oyster upward, through fishes, eels, serpents, quadrupeds, birds, quadrumana, or apes, to man. Man belongs to another kingdom, another department of God's works, more distinct from the highest brute than the highest brute is from a stone. Because it is always right, if politic, to kill a brute, it does not follow that it is ever right, under any conceivable circumstances, to take the life of a man. The two thoughts and acts are radically apart. If it be ever right to kill a man, it must be from entirely different motives from those which make it always right, if convenient, to kill a brute.

And just here, at this separating point, we reach the most fundamental thought connected with this commandment, "Thou shalt not kill." We may state it, perhaps, most successfully by instituting the inquiry, Why is it wrong to kill? On what principle, on what fact, or collection of facts, does the Almighty base this stern prohibition, "THOU SHALT NOT KILL?" This question may be primarily answered in a single statement, and then several secondary answers may be added.

It is primarily wrong to kill a man because he has an immortal soul, and because the destiny of this immortal soul is decided by his mortal life.

Now the fact that man has an immortal soul I shall not now argue, but shall assert. I believe it. You believe it. I believe that the Bible teaches it. You believe that the Bible teaches it.

This one fact makes a greater distinction between a brute and a man, than between a transient spark of fire and a star. "Who knoweth," says the book of Ecclesiastes, "the spirit of man that goeth upward, and the spirit of the beast that goeth downward to the earth?" The beast has a spirit. And it is a very mysterious thing, "Who knoweth it?" But it is a mere dull flash. It "goeth downward to the earth." It ebbs out with the blood. Knock the brute on the head and the spirit is gone. It is gone, perhaps never to reappear. The brute has no resurrection, more than the girdled tree or the uprooted plant. Whether it is absorbed into a great ocean of brute spirit, to crop out again in some other animal life, or not, it is impossible to determine. "Who knoweth?" It is not necessary for us to know, and as yet we have not learned. I do not know but that animals will always exist, even in heaven. I know just absolutely nothing about it. No man can prove that it will not be so. But I have no reason to believe that there will ever be any resurrection, any "standing again" of the individual spirit of a dead beast. There are no intimations of it in the Bible. There are no indications of it in present facts. They seem to have only an earthly life. There is no looking forward in their nature; no provisions for the future; no instinctive anticipations of it, no demand for it. They arise and fall, serve their purpose, all that they seem to be made for, and then pass away.

It is not so with man. Man has power to anticipate and desire an everlasting life. Ever and anon the glimmerings of eternity flash out from him. You take a caterpillar, or any other worm, and carefully dissect it in a certain stage of its growth, and you will find wrapped up in its texture the nascent form of another animal, the fly; and from that alone you might wisely anticipate that it was destined in due season to evolve from its substance in this other prefigured type of animal life. You watch it, and you will find that by and by, in its progress, it will wrap itself up in a covering, and in the form of a chrysalis lie down in sleep, and then will evolve from it in another stage of life, a fly. Now the anticipation of the butterfly is in the caterpillar; and God having created the anticipation, is bound by his wisdom, in due time, to evolve the thing promised. There the progress ends. God has not wrapped up in the butterfly any further anticipation, and consequently we expect no further development. The butterfly dies, and there is the end of it. There is no promised immortality in the spirit of a beast.

But God has wrapped up in man's soul an evident provision for and looking forward to another stage of life. And he is bound, therefore, in wisdom to give it. These intimations of immortality are universal. They form a part of all the false religions as well as of the true religion. They are seen in the fearfulness of remorse on the death-bed; in the patient endurance of suffering, hoping for future reward; and in the tombstones that mark the resting-place of the dead. The very question, "If a man die shall he live again?" indicates that he *will* live. For if not, if God has not made him for it, why does he ask the question? Why are we capable of conceiving the thought and cherishing the desire? And the instinctive answer to the inquiry is, "YES." And the ancient divine answer was, "All the days of my appointed time will I wait till my *change* come." Mark you, a CHANGE; not a cessation of being, but a CHANGE. Christ answers: "Marvel not, for verily, verily, I say unto you, the hour is coming when they that are in their graves shall hear his voice and come forth: they that have done good to everlasting life, and they that have done evil to everlasting damnation."

How fearful, then, it is abruptly to terminate the mortal life of an immortal being! He who interferes with the life of a man without just cause, usurps the prerogative of the Almighty. It is the highest possible robbery; it is the concentration and extreme of all injustice and wrong. All other acts of oppression and cruelty may be remedied, or compensated, or atoned for, at least partially; but for this there is no remedy, no atonement. A man's property may be restored, or he may subsist and achieve life's purpose as fully without it; a man's liberty lost may be given him again; a man's reputation, stabbed by the slanderer, may be regained, and he may shine the brighter for the temporary tarnish; but his life once gone is hopelessly, forever sacrificed. It is like "water spilled on the ground, that cannot be gathered again." No bittter remorse of the murderer can reanimate the lifeless body, or call back the soul. One thing only is more valuable than life, and that is, virtue, piety, God's stamp on the soul, a title to heaven; but that it is not in the power of one man either to give to or take from another. The very highest treasure, infinitely higher than all others, that one human being can possibly steal from another, and destroy, is LIFE. Satan was nearly right, as usual, when he said, "Skin for skin, yea, all that a man hath, will he give for his life." All but virtue may a man justly surrender for life.

And what terrible consequences may follow the premature loss of a life, in another world, it is impossible for us even to conjecture, because we know so little of the nature of the connection of the present life with the eternity to follow. By robbing a human being of life you may rob him of heaven, and commit an act for which the regret and remorse may be felt long after your present life shall end. The greatest criminal may reform; and you, by suddenly sending him to his account, with all his unforgiven sins upon his head, and without opportunity for repentance, may cut off his opportunity for mercy, and consign him to ruin and unending dismay.

The minor and secondary reasons why murder is forbidden are so inferior to this one grand reason, that it seems unnecessary even to mention them. I will, however, adduce a few. In proportion to the lowness of the estimation which a community entertain of the value of life does human life become uncertain. This engenders suspicion, timidity, jealousy, deception, cruelty, and a long catalogue of vices. See this evinced in some barbarian tribes. The Fijis, for instance, before their late Christianization, were strangely addicted to the crime of murder. All strangers were mercilessly killed, and on the slightest provocation life even among themselves was sacrificed. The consequence was that they all went, as all the heathen Fijis still go, constantly armed with murderous clubs. A man was always put on his self-defense. The women, being weaker, are treacherous and enslaved. A restless looking about characterizes the men whenever together. The slightest noise or alarm leads to the grasping and brandishing of the club, and often on the smallest provocation the feeble or the unguarded fall. Their insular seclusion from the rest of mankind has alone saved them from extirpation. Virtue is of course impossible in such a society, and were all human beings Fijis, man could never become civilized and noble, and ere long the earth would be denuded of its human population. What we see ripened among them is the inevitable effect of a low estimation of the value of human life.

Again, insecurity of human life, implies all minor insecurities. It necessitates anarchy and misrule. The greater includes the less. Where on a slight provocation life may be destroyed, property is not secure, character is not safe, rewards for integrity and virtue are not certain, and life is stripped of its genuine nobility.

It will thus be found, finally, that a strict obedience, from right motives, to the command, THOU SHALT NOT KILL, involves with it, almost as a necessity, an obedience to all the other commandments of God; while an undervaluation of human life brings with it, inevitably, sensuality, deception, fraud, idleness, vice of every kind, and ruin.

It may be deemed by some unnecessary, before a Christian congregation, to present this subject, but it is the duty of the minister to declare the whole counsel of God. And, my friends, it is fearful for us to consider that murder is by no means an uncommon crime in our country. This lowest depth of human guilt is not unfrequently reached. Seldom, indeed, does one who has read and listened to the word of God, who has joined in singing the praises of Christ in the sanctuary, or united with the congregation habitually in public prayer, reach this enormity of guilt; but even such cases are not unknown. And among the Sabbath-breaking and profane and intemperate part of the community, not unfrequently one and another is found who either passionately or treacherously, or sometimes maliciously, robs a fellow human being of his greatest treasure, life. And how shocking is the thought that many are deterred from it simply by a fear of detection, or by the absence of a malevolent disposition, and not from any belief in the preciousness of human life, not from any high and holy regard to the will of God. It is my duty as a minister of the Gospel to inculcate the right sentiment on this subject, and preach the infinite sacredness of human life.

And is it not worthy of thought that few find themselves suddenly betrayed into the greatest crimes? Vice is stealthy in its progress, beginning in the imagination, sometimes lurking and rioting there a long time before it ripens into action. God sees more murders than all mankind see. There are sometimes murders where there are no deaths. Hear the disciple whom Jesus loved, 1 John iii, 15: "Whosoever hateth his brother is a murderer: and ye know that no murderer hath eternal life abiding in him." Real, malignant hatred, that needs only opportunity to act, that would slay were it not for the danger of punishment; that is murder, for God looks at the heart. And every degree of this feeling is wrong, and tends to create still more. Hatred is a cancer; once fastened on the soul, it spreads till it eats out all eternal life. When Elisha the prophet met Hazael, the future wicked king, the prophet wept. Hazael inquired, "Why weepeth my lord?" And the prophet said it was because he saw the crimes that Hazael would hereafter commit. And when he described the murders which by vision he saw, Hazael indignantly exclaimed, "Is thy servant a dog that he should do this great thing?" And yet Hazael afterward did it.

Let it not, then, be thought superfluous that I explain the doctrine of God on the sacredness of human life. Remember, it is a commandment of God to all mankind, applying only to human beings, however young or however old, THOU SHALT NOT KILL.

The punishment inflicted upon this dreadful crime, even in the present life, is generally terrible. Few are so hardened as to be able to suppress the fires of hell that burn in the soul after the commission of murder. It has passed into a proverb that "murder will out." As Daniel Webster has well said, "Such a secret can be safe nowhere." "The whole creation of God has neither nook nor corner where the guilty can bestow it and say it is safe. Not to speak of that eye which glances through all disguises, and beholds everything as in the splendor of noon, such secrets of guilt are never safe: 'Murder will out.' True it is that Providence hath so ordained, and doth so govern all things, that those who break the great law of Heaven, by shedding man's blood, seldom succeed in avoiding discovery;" "the secret which the murderer possesses soon comes to possess him; and like the evil spirits of which we read, it overcomes him, and leads him whithersoever it will. He feels it beating at his heart, rising to his throat, and demanding disclosure. He thinks the whole world sees it in his face, reads it in his eyes, and almost hears its workings in the very silence of his thoughts. It has become his master; it betrays his discretion, it breaks down his courage, it conquers his prudence." "It must be confessed, it will be confessed; there is no refuge from confession but in suicide, and suicide is confession."

Some have argued from this commandment, that it is not right for the government to take the life of a human being as a criminal or in war. They assert that the state has no right to execute a murderer, because God has said, "Thou shalt not kill." This is a hasty and unwarrantable conclusion. It should be observed that the state must have power that cannot be given to an individual, and therefore many acts are right for a state that are not right for an individual. It is said, THOU SHALT NOT STEAL; but that does not forbid the state from imposing a fine upon a man as a punishment for crime, and if need be collecting it by force. A man has a right to personal liberty, but the state may justly take it away if the man is criminal and dangerous in society. So if a man has taken the life of another he has forfeited his right to liberty; and if he has forfeited his right to life it does not oppose the doctrine of this commandment. This commandment was made for men, and not for states. And even as a commandment for man it is subject, as all general precepts are, to modification in extraordinary circumstances. To protect life, either one's own or that of a friend, against murder, it is right in the sight of man and of God to sacrifice the life of the intended murderer. This has always been approved by the common instincts of humanity, and the judgment of the wise and good. Bible teaching and Bible example justify it.

To take human life, except when it is justly forfeited, is wrong, because we are to live forever. Our beloved friends that have gone before yet live. We shall meet them again. If the murderer shall meet his victim there, so, too, will those who have inflicted minor injuries meet their wronged ones there. The abused, the neglected, the oppressed will meet their insulters and oppressors there. O what terrible meetings! Ought we not to think of it? Life's reponsibilities cannot be thrown off even with our bodies. We cannot carry our money with us, but we can carry the wrongs and crimes and wickedness which that money has engendered. We must take our souls with us. We shall not need to carry our account-books, for our actions will be recorded in God's judgment-book. What lines are already written there! What lines are writing now!

It is wrong to shorten the life of a human being, because the present probationary existence is unutterably valuable to him. Even so, then, this life is unutterably valuable to us. Are we making it so? Are we using it as though it was valuable? Are we preparing our spirits for an upward flight? Are we the disciples of Christ? He says, "If any man is ashamed to confess me before men, of him will I be ashamed before my Father and the holy angels." Are any of us ashamed to confess him? Is it possible that any of us can consider this subject, the sacredness of human life, without applying it to ourselves thus: It is wrong to take the life of a human being. God has said, "Thou shalt not kill." It is not only wrong, therefore, for me to take the life of a human being, but it would be a terrible crime for any one short of God Almighty to take my life. But why? Why is my life of any value? Am I doing any good with it? Am I serving its great end? Am I so shaping it as to prepare for the bliss of heaven? Or am I tending downward?

God help you to decide that wisely and truly. If you are Christ's, rejoice? If not, seek salvation to-day, by giving yourselves to Christ.

VIII.

THE SIXTH COMMANDMENT.

• The Crime of Suicide.

THOU SHALT NOT KILL.—Exodus xx, 13.

THIS commandment directly forbids suicide, a crime more common than murder. This crime is generally caused by despair.

The weeping prophet Jeremiah, when all his earthly hopes were blasted, exclaimed, "It is good that a man should both hope, and quietly wait for the salvation of the Lord." There are many kinds of salvation, such as from poverty, sickness, disgrace, and death, as well as from eternal ruin. The salvation hoped for by Jeremiah was from earthly ruin. The author of Lamentations was what some would call a broken-hearted man. His prospects of success were all ruined and gone. Nothing was left to hope for; nothing but to die. He had belonged to a nation that was animated by a peculiar hope—the oldest and proudest nation of the world. Now it was conquered and destroyed. Its capital was broken down; its temple despoiled of its furniture; its king was a captive; its leading men and women slaves; its very language was a reproach, and its prophets, embracing himself, a by-word and a scoffing among the nations of the earth. What was there left for him to do? He could not become a Babylonian; he could not forget his mother tongue; he could not worship the idols of Assyria; his own God had not answered his prayers, and seemed to show no regard for him. What was there left for him but to die?

Had the weeping prophet put an end to his life, he would have done only what Hannibal and Cato and Brutus and many other heathens, in like circumstances, have done. But no. He wept, but his were not the tears of despair; he wrote his country's epitaph, but it was enlivened by the hope of a resurrection; he uttered the bitterest lamentations, but they were enlightened with the flashes of such faith as this: "It is good that a man should both hope, and quietly wait for the salvation of the Lord!" Such is the example of one who had a sound mind, and was cheered with faith in God.

I. I purpose in this discourse to show the wrongfulness of despondency, or the views that we should entertain of despair.

It might seem to some persons inappropriate to address an audience of young men on a wrongful habit of mind to which persons of their age are not inclined, but further observation would show them that despair is not confined to any age. Indeed it is, probably, quite as prevalent among the young as among the more advanced in years.

By despondency I mean that state of mind directly opposite to hope. It is an absence of exhilarating buoyancy of feeling. It is an expectation of disaster and defeat. It is a tendency to look on the dark side of things. It clothes the heavens and the earth in an unnatural blue. It makes its victims peevish and fretful. It fills the imagination with dismal forebodings. It gives a man the nightmare when awake and under self-control. The despondent man if engaged in business expects to fail. The price of the stock that he owns will certainly fall; his creditors will never pay; his debts will wreck him. Is he a farmer? The winter will certainly kill his wheat and his sheep; an early frost will destroy his corn; insects are much more destructive now than ever before; farming is the worst of all business, and never so bad as now. Is he a student? There is no prospect in this country for a well-educated man, quacks and charlatans take all the prizes; the people never see and acknowledge genuine merit; the ranks of the professions are all full; knowledge is becoming so universal now that it is no distinction, and its possession is of no value. Is he a minister? The world was never so wicked before. Good men are despised now; the proud and the hypocritical are exalted. Men prefer tinsel to gold; a little show is worth far more than solid merit. Aged ministers are like poor old horses turned out to die. Such will be my fate.

These are no fancy sketches. They are but surface skimmings of a deep, dark, blue sea of despondency, that rolls coldly over many a soul.

In looking at these cases many striking facts are to be observed.

1. As I have already intimated, there is no peculiar zone of age to which these dark clouds are confined. It is seldom that boys and girls, perhaps, exhibit or feel for any appreciable length of time this painful condition, except in a very few instances of unnatural precocity, produced by the modern hot-bed style of civilization. But after childhood is passed, early and later youth has its full proportion of despondent victims. As the years roll on many of them either die as a consequence of their low spirits, or learn better, and therefore the new cases occurring do not make the number any greater. Indeed I think that the proportion of hopeful, cheerful persons is decidedly greater among old people than among young people; for, perhaps, cheerful persons have the best pros-

pect of long life. Yet instances of despondency are not wanting in any age.

2. Again, observe that this habit of feeling is not affected perceptibly by condition, or rank, or prospects. The rich are, if there is any difference, more liable to it than the poor; the very rich than the very poor. The very strong and athletic do not escape; the feeble and pining sometimes do. Sometimes a poor man, toiling hard for his daily bread, is cheerful, while the inheritor of wealth groans and sighs amid all the luxuries that money can purchase. Genius is peculiarly exposed to despondency; education seems often to induce it.

3. Another remarkable characteristic of this evil is that it is intermittent. It is not exactly, like mysterious agues and fevers, a periodical visitant, coming at intervals of twenty-four or forty-eight hours, or other well-defined terms, but remittent, irregular, capricious. People subject to despondency have generally their seasons of great exhilaration. They keep up the equilibrium by fits of exultation. Perhaps this fact gave origin to the proverb,

"Great wit's to madness near allied."

Indeed it is a psychological fact of some interest, that many persons remarkable for wit, productive of great laughter in others, have been subject to almost uncontrollable despondency. Such was the case with Dean Swift, and Lamb, and Hood, and Hook; but such was not the case with Sydney Smith.

This disposition has sometimes been called the poetical temperament, because those who indulge the imagination are more than others inclined to excesses of joy and sorrow, to ecstacies of delight or despair. Instances of this are seen in Cowper and Byron and Goethe, and not unlikely in Alexander Smith and Tennyson. But this is far from being universal. Such men as Milton and Shakspeare and Gray and Wordsworth and Bryant and Longfellow and Whittier, are too wise and well rounded out in their mental nature to go, by turns, moping and complaining and leaping through life. If this be the poetical temperament it is the poetry of disease, not of health; it is the music of the dying swan, not of the living nightingale.

Akin to despondency, but deeper and darker in its hue, is despair. Despondency, I have said, is the exact opposite of hope; despair is the exact opposite of faith. The Bible says, "Hope is an anchor to the soul, sure and steadfast." In like manner desponding is a dead weight to the soul, like a water-logged vessel, constantly dragging its freight beneath the waves. The Bible says, "Faith is the substance of things hoped for, the evidence of things not seen."

The Bible here means *good things*. Faith is the very substance or foundation of all *good things* hereafter to be enjoyed. In like manner despair is the substance of *evil things* expected, the evidence of *evil things* not seen. Thus to us these are absolutely opposite passions: Hope and despondency, faith and despair. Hope is a great blessing, faith a greater blessing; yes, faith, in the Christian sense, is the greatest of all blessings.. Despondency is a great evil, despair greater; nay, despair is the greatest curse on earth or in hell.

No tongue can describe the horrors of despair. No artist can depict human lineaments sad enough to suggest one half of its woe. It is the absence of all good, the apprehension of all evil; and, inasmuch as expectation is often worse than fact, despair is worse than any agony of body or pain of soul, through positive evil, that could possibly be endured. Often it has paralyzed the brain and chilled the very heart. The best gift of God is faith; the very crisis and completion of evil is despair.

What a sad thought it is that despondency, at least in its incipient advances, has so many victims. Could we see them together what a collection of wretches should we behold! What a dead sea of human souls! How upon looking at them should we be inclined, with Voltaire, to exclaim, "The world contains carcasses rather than men, and I wish that I had never been born!" or better, with Jeremiah, "O that my head were waters," etc.

II. Having observed the nature of these terrible kindred evils, despondency and despair, which differ from each other in intensity only, as the storm differs from the tornado, let us inquire into their origin. What causes despondency? What causes despair?

When we speak of causes, various ideas may be suggested. We may inquire into the *final* cause, thus: Why did God make the human soul capable of despair? This is a mysterious question, and only one of a general class. Why did God make man capable of pain? What is the use of pain? What motive in God caused him to create the capability of pain in man? Why may that which produces the most exquiite pleasure produces the most excruciating pain? The eye in delirium tremens, the ear, the whole brain? I do not know, except that the possibility of pain seems to us to be necessary to make the posibility of pleasure. There can be no day without the possibility of night; no peace without the possibility of disturbance; no order without the possibility of anarchy; no hope without the possibility of despondency; no faith without the possibility of despair.

As Wordsworth well says:

O life! without thy checkered scene
Of right and wrong, of weal and woe,
Success and failure, could a ground
For magnanimity be found?
For faith 'mid ruined hopes serene?
Or whence could virtue flow?

Pain entered through a ghastly breach—
Nor while sin lasts must efforts cease;
Heaven upon earth's an empty boast;
But, for the bowers of Eden lost,
Mercy has placed within our reach
A portion of God's peace.

But what are the efficient causes of despondency or despair? What are its invariable antecedents, which, knowing, we may guard against them?

First, they may be bodily.

Some of these bodily causes are organic, or originate with the constitution. The ancient physiologists divided all human beings into four classes, according to the temperament, which they called the *sanguine*, the *melancholic*, the *choleric*, and the *phlegmatic*. Modern physiologists add another class, the *nervous*, making five. Persons of the melancholic temperament have either a sluggish circulation of the blood, or an excess of bile, or some abnormal action of the brain, which brings them constantly into a physical condition similar to that diseased state which produces in sleep painful dreams, and in wakefulness moroseness, unsociableness, and a tendency to despair.

Those who have been of this temperament have in their happiest moments eloquently eulogized its advantages. Dr. Martyn Paine says: "The melancholic is the man of men. I had almost said, in moral constitution, he is perpetuated, unchanged, from the model of his race. Here is witnessed the highest intellectual renown at the very dawn of manhood; and here it is that we often meet with genius struggling with those adversities which arrest the ambition of other temperaments." "This imagination, therefore, is of the highest order, being disciplined by the sterner faculties. It is such an imagination as is always an element of genius; such as contemplates the realities of life and the truths of revelation. He is thoughtful, grave, or sad, but may tune his mind to great elevation, and great sublimity and enthusiasm, and often soars on poetic wings through the regions of heaven." Elsewhere he says: "Hence it is that hypochondriacism and insanity are apt to supervene on the melancholic temperament."

Sometimes the bodily condition tending to despondency, instead of being a temperament, or an organic abnormal condition, is a temporary disease, having its beginning, its tendency to a crisis, and a cure; sometimes it becomes chronic and habitual.

Sometimes its victims not only become accustomed to it, but even learn to take a sort of pleasure in it. Men may be so habituated to pain as to feel unnatural and unhappy if they are relieved from it, just as the human body may become so inured to poison as to seem to require it. Some men would be still more unhappy than they are, seemingly, if they could not fret and complain and render others unhappy. Such is the power of habit; such also is often the wonderful influence which the body exerts over the soul.

Of course, so far as despondency is caused by bodily condition, it can be remedied primarily by medicine and proper regimen and diet, which is one of the most valuable departments of physiological science. In its incipient stages the unhappy sufferer can, if he understands his own difficulty, seek the aid of a physician, and often obtain relief. Precisely where self-control and responsibility cease, and what may properly be called insanity begins, is a very delicate question, and one which I do not propose now to investigate.

2. Despondency is often caused by irregular habits and intemperance. Every stimulus is followed by reaction. The miserable opium-eaters, though occasionally one lives to a good old age, are generally wrecked into idiocy, impotency, and an early death. Habitual drink-

ers of alcohol, in proportion to the strength and frequency of their potations, are the victims of fancied sorrows and indescribable wretchedness in the intervals of their intoxication. Disorder of every kind induces despondency.

3. Another prolific source of this trouble is idleness. Labor is not a curse; it is a blessing. The curse pronounced upon Adam was not labor, but the sterility of the earth and its production of weeds. Even mental toil is rewarded more by the health and joy it engenders than by its result. This is true also of bodily toil. God works. Incessant benevolent activity is his nature. So man should work. An idle person is either imbecile, an undeveloped human being, or the victim of wretchedness.

4. I need not dwell upon the consequences of sudden disappointments, severe bereavements, great afflictions. There are many persons who are not able to bear sudden and violent shocks of sorrow. The loss of property, the loss of friends, the loss of reputation, have sometimes prostrated their victims at a blow, and hurled them into incurable despair. When, through the connection of the soul with the body, the shock is followed by a physiological change, sometimes the difficulty is incurable; but if confined to the soul, such is the wonderful elasticity of human nature, the crushed spirit revives, and soon again puts forth the tender

shoots of hope, ere long to blossom into joy and ripen into peace. No man is thoroughly disciplined, and the subject of the largest Christian faith, who is not able to rally from any earthly shock. Job said in his calamity, "Though he slay me, yet will I trust in him;" and Jeremiah well said, "It is good that a man should both hope and quietly wait for the salvation of the Lord."

5. I am constrained to believe that the greatest source of low spirits, especially among educated and refined persons, is the want of the true Christian religion.

Infidelity is essentially and necessarily productive of dissatisfaction. This is true theoretically, and true practically. It can be demonstrated to the reason; it can be illustrated by history; it can be confirmed by almost every person, to some extent, by his own experience.

Infidelity is a want of faith in what ought to be regarded as the stable pillars of the universe. How can a man be happy in a building that may fall into ruins and destroy him in an instant? Is there any pleasure in being deprived of faith in God? In supposing one's self to be a mere outgrowth of matter, like a fungus? What is there desirable in reason, if it shall expire to-morrow? What in imagination, if it must be tied to a hundred and fifty pounds of earth and water, to be melted into vulgar dirt, and disappear forever in a few days? What is there pleasant in supposing that all the best of men have been deceived, and are now nothing, and soon we shall be like them, only not deceived?

But I need not reason on the matter. Facts prove it. Irreligious men are generally discontented. Especially does this apply to men who are determinately hostile to Christianity. There is a secret as well as an open history to such men. There are hours of sorrow and repining and dissatisfaction never described. Solitude is wretchedness to the man who has no hope in God; meditation is madness, sober thought is pain. The autobiographies and letters and conversations of rejecters of divine revelation demonstrate this assertion.

III. Allow me, then, to show you what is the proper and only efficient remedy for despondency in its full fruit of despair.

I have already said that so far as it is the result of physical organization or disease, it must be reached and overcome largely through medical means, though the wisest of physicians now appreciate the fact that the body can often be benefited most through the mind. It is also evident that all intemperance and irregularities of living must be avoided if we would escape this sorrow.

But the most effectual and only sovereign remedy is Christian faith, Christian experience, and Christian character. This—for the three elements constitute but one possession—is offered to all, and is attainable by all; and, so far as it is attained, directly nullifies and annihilates despondency.

Carlyle once said, "Christianity is the religion of sorrow." Carlyle never wrote a greater falsehood; and he has written as great if not as many falsehoods as any other writer of the present generation in our language. His views of human nature in general, of government and society, and of men, are false. Born of Christian parents, he inherited much of the genuine Scotch integrity and manliness which only a Christian education could give, and which gave him some attractiveness in his early life; but having rejected the actual Christian experience and life of his fathers, he has been a giant floundering in the mud of metaphysics, uttering strange doctrines and mystifying what is simple, perverting the truth, and battling with fancied foes in the dark, all his life; and his career threatens to end in pernicious fault-finding and despair. Christianity is not a religion of sorrow. Christ, indeed, was a man of sorrows; but he changed his sorrows into triumphs, his pain into joy. And, moreover, his sorrow and his pain were designed to bless the whole world.

And this is the great power of Christianity, that it takes real sorrow and makes it sooner or later productive of real joy. Sorrow and affliction, if they come to a Christian, are by the mysterious chemistry of the Gospel converted into *character*, into excellence, into eternal good.

The religion of Christ makes no new sorrow. It discloses some evil that before was unknown, but it immediately provides a remedy. Its very center and substance is love. Is there any pain in love? "The fruit of the Spirit is love, joy, peace, long-suffering, gentleness, meekness, patience, temperance." Is there any sorrow in them?

The true Christian cannot despair. He ought never to despond.

But I hear the practical objection, that many professed Christians are seemingly unhappy, discontented, and even despondent. "Why is this, if Christianity is peaceful, and even joyous?"

It is because professed Christians are not informed as to their duty. Preachers dwell too much upon doctrine, too little upon life. They forget that their function is to be preachers of the GOSPEL. Gospel is another word that needs to be demagnetized before it can be understood. Gospel is a good spell, a good story or announcement, or good news. Good news has no tendency to make men despondent, unless they are determined to reject it. The Gospel is an announcement of immortality, of the essential and everlasting integrity of virtue and love of God. Whoever receives the Gospel is comforted, enlightened, elevated, cheered.

It is a positive sin for a Christian to cultivate or indulge morbid despondency. He thereby dishonors the Saviour and robs God. When men come to see it as a sin they will not boast of it, but rather contend against it, and use means for its removal, and pray to be delivered from it.

A good practical remedy for despondency is to make efforts to live a Christian life, even though destitute of hope and faith. It is related of a wealthy man of Paris, that being desolate and alone, having exhausted all the gratifications of society, and being unstrung in soul and body, and weary of life, he finally resolved, on one dark and dreary night of winter, to put an end to his life. He accordingly made all the preparations, left his house and walked toward the river Seine, with a full purpose of casting himself into the water. On approaching the bank he observed a poor miserably clad woman with two children stealthily creeping down toward the bank, evidently trying to elude the vigilance of the police. His curiosity was excited, and he inquired of her what she was doing. He learned that she, too, was weary of life. She was one of the victims of a stern iron civilization, which

Rousseau justly thought is worse than the savage state. Her two children were starving for want of food, and she had eaten nothing for several days. No virtuous way of obtaining a livelihood was opened to her, and she was now about to end her own life and her children's. The rich hypochondriac's heart was touched. Here, said he, is real misery, greater than mine. I am about to die by my own act, but this woman and her children need not die. I have money enough, and will supply their wants. The result was that he commenced a course of benevolent life from that time, and many years afterward died in an honorable old age, after a long career of benevolent usefulness, followed to the grave by many who had been comforted and blessed by his Christian benevolence.

The practical part of Christianity is to many much easier than the theoretical. I am liberal enough to suppose that Christ recognizes as his followers many whom some Churchmen call infidels. What Christ desires is a right spirit; not merely a right belief. "Master," said the disciples once, "we saw one casting out devils in thy name, but he follows not with us, and we rebuked him." Hear the reply of the Master: "Forbid him not: for there is no man which shall do a miracle in my name, that can lightly speak evil of me. For he that is not against us is on our part."

When I see a man striving honestly to live a correct life, reverent toward God, approving the good, shrinking from and contending against evil, though from some peculiar education he may differ widely from me in opinion, and in the expression of opinion, I cannot believe that Christ does not approve and will not reward that honesty of purpose and fidelity of character.

This door to a Christian character is open wide to all.

I cannot close this discourse without adding a word cognate to the subject which has engaged our attention, upon the question whether, under any circumstances, it is allowable for a Christian to put an end to his own life.

You will notice the form of the question: Whether it is *right for a Christian* to commit suicide? Those who have not received Christian information and education are to be judged according to the light which they have. This is in harmony with the tenor of Scripture. The heathen were compelled to consider this subject by the light of nature, and are not to be held responsible to our standard.

In considering this question, observe, first, that the Bible describes no instance of suicide by a thoroughly good man, and no instance in which it seems to be commended or justified. Samson consented to slay himself with his enemies. The miserable Saul, first king of

Israel, when hopelessly defeated, and overcome by remorse and despair, prayed another man to take his life, but dared not himself commit the act. David in all his troubles seemed never to dream of it. Job, in his superhuman sorrows, is not represented as even tempted of Satan to end his life. In the New Testament, of all who ever professed love to Christ, Judas alone was led to perish by his own hands.

Suicide is directly opposed to the fundamental principles of Christianity, which are, that this life is designed to furnish opportunity to prepare for another, and that, therefore, this life is inexpressibly valuable, and is never to be terminated except by the appointment of God.

Sorrow must be borne heroically, and with patience, because it is the material of endless joy. "I reckon that the sufferings of this present time are not worthy to be compared with the glory that shall be revealed in us." "For these light afflictions, which are but for a moment, work out for us a far more exceeding and eternal weight of glory; while we look not at the things which are seen, but at the things which are not seen; for the things which are seen are temporal, but the things which are not seen are eternal."

The man who believes this cannot be permanently unhappy. The disease is conquered; the temptation is crushed out.

Christianity teaches us that the great object of human life is usefulness, and the opportunity for usefulness never ends.

Milton well expresses his thought in that sublime sonnet which he wrote on his own blindness:

"When I consider how my life is spent,
Ere half my days, in this dark world and wide,
And that one talent which is death to hide,
Lodged with me useless, though my soul were bent
To serve therewith my Maker, and present
My true account, lest he returning chide;
Doth God exact day labor, light denied?
I fondly ask; but patience, to prevent
That murmur, soon replies, God doth not need
Either man's work or his own gifts; who best
Bear his mild yoke, they serve him best; his state
Is kingly; thousands at his bidding speed,
And post o'er land and ocean without rest;
They also serve who only stand and wait."

How nobly did Milton more than verify this truth in his own experience. Look at that noble scholar so terribly afflicted in the very prime of his career. Remember his course of life. He was bred as a Christian scholar from his childhood; early taught to pray and praise God. At the age of sixteen he entered college; and at the age of twenty-three he graduated master of arts, and left the university, and then spent five years more in rigid orderly reading and study, occasionally for recreation writing some short productions in poetry and prose. This brought him to the age of thirty, when he spent nearly two years in travel. All this time he cherished an ambition of writing a poem of a moral and Christian character, that should for all time to come honor God and bless man. It was a wonderful ambition. For this he read, meditated, observed, and studied. At the age of thirty-two the great political troubles of the English revolution broke out, comparable to the American civil war, and Milton, though a retired scholar, was forced to enter the lists. He was a Republican and a Puritan, and brought his vast mental stores and thorough mental discipline to bear in the production of some of the noblest essays and treatises extant in human language. The great doctrine of universal toleration of conscience he first announced, which alone should make his name immortal. For fifteen long years he toiled, the most conspicuous man in England, except perhaps Cromwell; probably, so far as we can estimate, the most useful man in the world. But then came the terrible blow. His eyesight at forty-five was wholly gone. And shortly, as if to prove that evils never come singly, but in battalions, a counter-revolution was effected; he was outlawed, and compelled to live in seclusion and in domestic trouble. Pain, disease, obloquy, blindness, overwhelmed him. What would you expect of him but despair? Had he sunk down into premature old age, a broken-hearted man, the world would not have wondered; had he ended his own life, he would have died as nobly as Cato, Brutus, or even Demosthenes! But still he would have been a coward. But no; he knew too well the Christian doctrine: "They serve God who fly o'er sea and land; they also serve who stand and wait!" He was content, if God asked it, to stand and wait; and soon he found that, standing and waiting, he could be useful still; and the blind man, excluded from the world of colors and outward sights, saw within, heaven, paradise, earth, hell, and heaven again, and gave to the world, from his own soul, a panorama of vision and thought that has ennobled his mother tongue, and clothed the sublime story of man's Paradise Lost and Regained with the undying glory of poetic speech.

If there be one truth which every man should know, it is this: Christianity protests that to the Christian there is, there can be no such thing as evil. What men call evil is to the Christian always converted into good. Therefore the Christian should never despair. Least of all should he interfere with the regular current of his own life, which it is the prerogative of God alone to guide.

If, then, we are determined to be Christians, let us adopt these maxims in their fullest extent: *Nil desperandum est*, We must never despair; *Dum spiro, spero*, While I breathe, I hope.

"I cannot always trace the way,
Where thou, Almighty One, dost move;
But I can always, always say
That God is love.

"When mystery clouds my darkened path,
I'll check my dread, my doubts reprove;
In this my soul sweet comfort hath,
That God is love.

"Yes, God is love! a thought like this
Can every gloomy thought remove,
And turn all tears, all woes to bliss;
For God is love."

IX.

THE SEVENTH COMMANDMENT.

Marriage and its Duties.

THOU SHALT NOT COMMIT ADULTERY.—Exodus xx, 14.

THERE is no doubt about the meaning and nature of marriage with those who accept the teachings of the Bible. It is true that the practice of good men in the earliest days, which seems even to have been sanctioned by the Lord, was in violation of some of the highest requirements of marriage; and this fact is just mysterious enough not only to puzzle the devout Christian, and furnish to the caviler a good field to revel in, but also to compel all true Christians to discriminate for themselves, by a positive act of the will, between good and evil. The Bible does not remove all mysteries. We must still walk by faith, and not by sight.

Marriage is a divine institution. It is the design of God, our Maker, that human beings should live in families, the head of each of which should be a man and woman, united for life in an intimate union, existing between them alone, and excluding others, indissoluble but by death, or by such crime on the part of one as renders the union useless or injurious. This is taught in the Bible.

Adam and Eve were the first to illustrate the divine idea of matrimony. In the scriptural account of its origin it is briefly described as a union existing only between two, and to be perpetual. Adam is represented as saying, "Therefore shall a man leave his father and his mother, and shall cleave unto his wife; and they shall be one flesh." Gen. ii, 4. Jesus Christ quotes these words as coming from the Creator, and interprets them as sanctioning only a life-long union between one husband and one wife. This is the uniform teaching of the New Testament. This is God's type of marriage.

Whatever God approves is invariably found productive of good, and what he disapproves, of evil.

Moreover, the results of a strict adherence to the laws of matrimony are found to be beneficial to the individual, to the family, and to society; while disobedience to them degrades the individual, breaks up or disgraces families, and weakens a nation. Thus by rewards and retributions God confirms his word.

I. Let us consider first the benefits of marriage.

1. In approaching this subject let me again remind you of the supreme importance of the individual man, according to the Christian mode

of thinking. Human philosophy almost invariably sinks the individual and exalts the mass. It looks upon man arithmetically, and, because a million counts more than one, infers that one is of but little value, and that to effect anything we must aim to reach the million rather than the one. Christ, on the other hand, viewed each man as an infinite quantity; and when we reach infinite quantities arithmetic is no longer available. What Christ sought was to bless individuals, knowing that if *they* were perfected, institutions—which grow out of them—would necessarily be good.

Now matrimony, considered as a custom or practice of human beings, is the greatest possible blessing to the individuals affected by it, and through its benefit on individuals it blesses societies and the state.

It benefits the individual, first, by communicating to the individual a permanency of disposition and a stability of character such as no other institution can create.

The child is bound to the parents by dependence and affection until capable of sustaining himself; but even this relation would be uncertain and often broken but for the stable matrimony of the parents; and when the child reaches the age of youth he is isolated and solitary, having only the temporary connections of friendship and of business, which are soon found to be of little permanent influence. Matrimony stamps a life-long character upon the individual.

It is a glorious epoch in the life of a human being when he acquires a character that shall abide. Death itself cannot in all respects nullify the relations into which he enters by marriage. The volatile becomes fixed, ambitions are centered, hopes are steadied; from the dependent child, or the uncertain aspirant, he is exalted into one of the pillars of society, one of the independent component parts for whose good the whole fabric is regulated and sustained. This is all condensed into the Scripture expression, "For this cause shall a man leave his father and mother, and cleave unto his wife." Here, as usual, the masculine noun is intended to include both sexes. It is not only true that the man leaves father and mother, but also the woman shall leave father and mother and cleave to her husband; both become one. The old parental relation abides, it is true, in its memories, in its affection, but not in its mutual support and dependence. The relation of son and daughter is now overbalanced by the new and stronger one of husband and wife. This is to abide till death. Marriage is the first, if not the only relation of one human being to another, that without change is to *abide*.

2. In addition to the stability of character

communicated by matrimony, the parties thus united find in it a relation best constituted—for God is its author—to develop in them the highest individual excellence, and to fit them for the highest usefulness to others. "It is not good," or it is not the perfect condition for either man or woman, "to be alone."

The obvious effects upon body and mind, upon the affections and whole character, I must simply pronounce beneficial, without taking the time to explain and prove the assertion. But its social and national influences may with propriety be illustrated. The male and female, in their affections, instincts, and influences, reciprocally sustain and perfect each other. How elevating is the influence of strict, scriptural, permanent matrimony upon the children of the family thus constitnted. The mother teaches the children to honor the father whom she honors as husband, and the father teaches them to love the mother whom he loves as wife. Nothing but death should sunder this relation.

3. It is also natural, as the spontaneous outgrowth of the soul, that the parents of families should be interested in the common character of others around them, with whom their children will associate. This is the origin of public spirit, of public enterprise, of patriotism. The household is the mother of the state. A state is strong, and less exposed to revolutions, in

proportion to the perfection of the family relation maintained by the people. The country most noted in all the world for revolutions is also most noted for setting at defiance the seventh commandment.

The Church, too, is the natural out-growth of the family. But for the marriage relation, strictly obeyed, there would be no Church, no Sabbath-school, no Sabbath; no family prayer, no social prayer, no public prayer; no home subordination arising from mutual love, and therefore no voluntary, cheerful subordination to public authority; no order, no culture. Marriage is the contract which creates the world. But for it society would be resolved into chaos.

I speak of perfect marriage among perfect men and women. Of course it is seldom seen in anything like a perfect form. But we must look at the genuine type as it ought to be, and we should aim to make it what it ought to be.

II. The benefits of matrimony may be more distinctly seen by noticing the consequences of its neglect or violation.

Now, if it be true that God is the author of matrimony, by creating human beings for it, and adapted to it, and by commanding it in his word, then we may suppose that all deviations from its scriptural type will be seen to be injurious.

1. The first deviation from it is voluntary celibacy. This, so far from being forbidden, is recognized, and under some circumstances commanded in the Bible. Though the Church, in the dark ages, pressed this doctrine into extravagant and pernicious results, yet it cannot honestly be denied that the Bible commends those who, under certain circumstances, deny themselves the advantages of matrimonial relations, that they may devote themselves without incumbrance to some high mission for the good of their fellow-men. And it cannot be denied that by the blessed principle of compensation, which runs through the entire economy of the universe, those who are unmarried may, if they preserve a pure character, accomplish peculiar good and enjoy a peculiar reward. But the conditions must be maintained, otherwise they sin against God and their own souls.

Involuntary celibacy, or celibacy assumed as a badge of a class, binding its members against matrimony, has proved productive of great evils. This is a great error of that sect calling itself the Roman Catholic Church. History abundantly proves that it has corrupted the priesthood and the inmates of nunneries, diseasing the mind and engendering unholy ambitions, and unfitting them for those natural and correct sympathies which are needful in a religious teacher. God's laws cannot be broken with impunity.

Except in rare instances, such as those mentioned by the Saviour in Matthew xix, 10–12, celibacy should not be chosen. And where it is chosen, or seems to be providentially appointed, it should be sacredly employed to promote the higher interests of the Church for the good of our fellow-men.

2. Another deviation from matrimony is seen in polygamy. This was not, for a time, in the history of the world, expressly forbidden, in so much of the Bible as man then enjoyed. It was tolerated for a season among the Hebrews, because from their low mental and moral culture, and especially from the want of the general education of woman, it seemed to be the least of necessary evils. Good men, or those in the main approved by God, were allowed to have a plurality of wives. Christ abolished this law, which was temporary, and not intrinsically good. He expressly stated that "in the beginning it was not so." It was allowed on account of "the hardness of their hearts." Even among them it produced its inevitable results—degrading women, alienating the affections of children, and as the people advanced in mental and moral culture, exciting the disapprobation of the wise and pure.

It should be remembered that the light was

then dim. All the world was idolatrous but a very few. The Israelites were governed more by law than by knowledge. By an ignorant people a perfect law will not be obeyed; and it may be better to regulate disobedience than to have it promiscuous and disorderly. This at least was done by divine authority, before the light of Christianity had shone. But now, since we have the history of Christ, the doctrines of Christ, and the accomplished fact of redemption, and of the establishment of the Church, that principle is obsolete, at least so far as matrimony is concerned.

Polygamy, though temporarily tolerated in those dark times, when all the world were idolaters except a people living in a country smaller in size than several of our single states, is nevertheless wrong. It is always productive of evil. It is justly forbidden by every Christian state. It ought to be forbidden by law in our whole country; and when the rebellion engendered by slavery is fully suppressed, it will be the duty of the nation to see that the fundamental laws of marriage are observed in Utah, as a condition of receiving the protection of the general government, or any place or share in the councils of the nation.

3. Matrimony is also violated by perverting the union into a temporary contract terminable at pleasure. This is indirectly brought about

by too great facilities of divorce, and has been commended by opposers of the Bible, in later times, under the name, already disgraceful, of "free love."

This is no new theory. It is as old as sin, and its author is Satan. It has had its advocates ever since infidelity began, and it has been tested in large nations, and long enough to destroy whole communities and races. Free love! Why it is nothing but another name for the promiscuous destruction of families and degradation of individuals, that has been practiced by the vilest and meanest of human beings from time immemorial, but never found any body to commend it till there sprung up the infidels of modern times!

I can but pronounce the carrying out of this theory a direct violation of the seventh commandment. To degrade marriage into a mere civil contract, or bargain, to be observed so long as both parties might choose, and to be annulled by mutual consent, would effectually destroy the Bible idea of matrimony. It would destroy that permanency of which I spoke as the chief excellence of the institution. It would inevitably substitute caprice for law, and open the way for confusion, immorality, and licentiousness.

The arguments adduced for this irreligious practice are, that marriages often prove unhappy from incompatibility of disposition, that its restraints are burdensome and injurious, and that other unions would be more agreeable and profitable. Those who advocate this free and easy practice have much to say of "love" and "affinity," and "the marriage of the soul," and "legalized crime," and other high-sounding epithets, with which they attempt to sugarcoat vice and dishonor virtue.

In reply to them I do not hesitate to acknowledge that many married people are unhappy, and perhaps are rendered more so by their union. This, however, does not often arise from the marriage, but from the wickedness of the individuals themselves, by which they pervert that union, as other good things, into evil. Marriage will not necessarily make a miser generous, or a selfish man amiable, or a proud man courteous, or a vain man agreeable, or a profane man devout. Vice must produce its fruit. Nor would a divorce from the contract change the character of either party, or lessen the aggregate of evil in the community. If in some cases it would promise to relieve the good and generous from a life-long contact with the evil and selfish, it should be remembered that it is not often the good and virtuous that seek thus to be relieved. They are aware that virtue shines the brighter when the more fiercely tried. They know something of the compensations of virtue. They know that there is an internal as well as an external history. And though there may be an external conflict, there shall, if faithful, be an internal reward. The instruction of the Apostle Paul to husbands and wives converted from heathenism, while the other parties remained idolators, illustrates the principles of matrimony. "If any brother hath a wife that believeth not, and she be pleased to dwell with him, let him not put her away. And the woman which hath a husband that believeth not, and if he be pleased to dwell with her, let her not leave him." 1 Cor. vii, 12, 13. And this, too, was written to a people living in a heathen land, where divorce was easy and common, and where of course the people were immoral and weak. If the idolatrous parties availed themselves of this practice, and left their husbands or wives, the apostle had nothing to say to them, though, even in such a case, he did not give the Christian parties thus left any permission to marry again; and in no case did he permit a Christian to abandon wife or husband on account of the idolatry of the other party. Rather he exhorted them so to live as, if possible, to save the unbelieving husband or wife.

This oldest human institution, first established after the creation of man, provided for in the very nature of body and soul, existing in man's innocency, and only survivor of man's fall, is akin to those very laws of nature which are but expressions of the will of God, particularly in this—its permanency and indissolubility, while the parties to be affected by it still live.

God's laws derive their greatest power from their inflexibility. The necessity for food and raiment, for shelter and warmth, for labor and sleep, for fresh air and cleanliness, for exercise and mutual regard, often subject us all to great inconvenience and positive suffering. They often accomplish much evil. Not a summer passes without sun-strokes, not a winter without freezing some persons to death, not a spring without breeding consumptions, not an autumn without dysenteries, not a seed-time or harvest without excessive labor and disappointment. Generals and armies have lost battles because they could not fight longer without sleep; ships have gone down, with Christian missionaries on board, because they were not strong enough to resist the winds or waves; and churches, if struck by lightning, burn as quick as grog-shops and gambling saloons. And yet it is better that all these things should happen than that God's permanent laws of nature should be broken. This unchangeableness of God's laws, with all the undeniable long catalogue of evils that it produces, is yet an infinite blessing. Were God's laws capricious, the catalogue of evils would be a million-fold, yes, infinitely, greater. Men are made active, watchful, alert, vigorous, and steady by them. Now marriage is designed to accomplish the same end. Its benefits are designed to counterbalance its evils a thousand-fold, and the greater part of its benefits cannot be secured except on the understanding that it is like a natural relation, permanent and inflexible, except on the few conditions according to which it may be rightly annulled.

No man can estimate the disciplinary power it has thus exerted. How, by communicating steadiness to those united by its silken bonds, relieving them from all further interest in the thoughts preliminary to its adoption, and giving to them an object for steady industry in promoting each other's welfare and the good of children, attaching them to society, awakening a desire for property and the comforts of a permanent home, and begetting an interest in country and in the Church, and in forming permanent, domestic habits, it has shed the sunlight of paradise over this sinful world, no tongue can describe, no mind can comprehend. Now all these blessings are weakened precisely in proportion as the marriage tie is loosened. Those, therefore, if any such there be, who have reason to believe that in their special instances it is not what they hoped, or what in other circumstances it might be, have this assurance, that by faithfulness to the compact they bless society and bless the world; and such is God's great goodness and wisdom, that whatever tribute any man or woman renders heartily to virtue and right will never fail, in the end, of a full and glorious reward.

4. In enumerating the violations of this compact, and the methods of breaking this seventh commandment, I must mention another subject, exceedingly disagreeable to allude to out of the family circle, and especially before a Christian audience. And yet you will bear with me, for you expect faithfulness; and you are well aware that those who really love purity can look at vice for a warning and without contamination. I allude to that social vice which has produced, and is fostered by, the most degraded class of human beings that live on the face of the earth, found, alas! in all large cities, and not absent, perhaps, from a single city in this or any other land. How pitiable it is that so many human beings, created for immortality, with all those noble instincts and passions fitting them either for high usefulness in single life, if that should be their calling, or for the holy offices of wives and mothers, should be prostituted to shame and vice, to loss of self-respect, to intemperance, and bodily pain, and mental agony, crowded generally into a short and

hopeless life, and both punitively and mercifully shortened by an early death. True it is the most of history is unwritten. Who shall describe the tears and wailings, interspersed with drunken and insane hilarity, of those who, cut off from virtuous society, betake themselves to vice for a livelihood, and thenceforward live only to keep the passage-way to hell open, and exact toll from those who plunge into its depths!

Much sickly sentimentality is displayed by pseudo-philanthropists of modern times, who declaim against the injustice of Christian society, and especially of virtuous women, in severely refusing to open their doors and their hearts to intimacy with the fallen and vicious of their own sex. I have no apology to plead for those who will not put forth kind and strenuous efforts, like Christ, to save the fallen and win them to repentance and life; but I believe that a true penitent will not desire at once to be treated as though she had never broken the covenant of pure society; and I believe also that the instincts of virtuous woman, higher and nobler than the lower reason, in which perhaps man excels, teaches her that it is not proper to pass lightly over that guilt which stabs society in its most vulnerable and vital part, and tends to destroy all that exalts woman above the condition of a slave or a brute. Therefore it is that virtuous woman shrinks from tolerating vice in one of her own sex, to whom God has in a special sense committed the trust to maintain domestic purity and honor.

And since we must look at this painful subject, allow me to urge that Christianity has produced and is producing its exalting influence on the domestic purity of man. The ancient heathen nations, as is proved by the scanty descriptions of them extant, were full of licentiousness. This in many instances proved their final and utter ruin. Our own nation is to a large extent unchristian and infidel. A large portion of our population are seldom seen in churches, and are foes to the religion of Christ. They supply the avenues to moral and spiritual death. They throng our places of vicious amusement. They go from the drinking-holes to haunts of vice and down to ruin. There are millions who are better taught, and never disregard the teachings of pious mothers and fathers, and of the house of God. These are the hope of our country. They are our hope physically. They will not become poisoned with the deadly virus which God, in mingled justice and mercy, has caused to spring up from licentious vice. They will not transmit to their children feebleness and decay, dooming the innocent ones to premature death, that their families may become mercifully extinct. Depend upon it God is the defender of righteousness, and mightily will show it. His judgments are fearfully denounced against those who break his laws, and they will be inflicted.

Chastity is precious in man and woman. It preserves both mind and heart in purity, capable of appreciating in the highest degree the impulses of a virtuous ambition. It secures a healthy self-respect and a preparation for the domestic piety.

III. Marriage is chosen in the Bible as an illustration of the holiest union conceivable, even that between Christ and the Church. There is a depth of meaning in this figure, and in the scriptural passages describing it, that none but a mature Christian and a pure mind can appreciate. Adultery is also the figure chosen by the old prophets to describe the apostacy of the people, once enlightened and his worshipers, but now apostatized and rebellious. It is a fearful figure.

The Scriptures plainly inform us that this vice leads inevitably to all other sin. It ruins the whole man. It saps the very heart of virtue. It generates atheism, falsehood, blasphemy, shamelessness. It obliterates the conscience, leaving only its remorse. The law of right is gone. Delight in purity is gone. A correct taste is gone. Manhood is gone. Nothing but a radical repentance and reform and true regeneration will save, and the scars of the wounds will not disappear in the present life.

Our view of this subject would be very incomplete if we forgot the instruction of Christ on this subject. He places the commission of the crime in the heart; as we should now say, in the intention. Not merely in thought, involuntary and uncherished; not merely in passion, uncontrollable in its inception; but in intention, though it be restrained only by fear or inability. Heed, then, the instruction of the Bible: "Keep thy heart with all diligence, for out of it are the issues of life." "As a man thinketh so is he." The reading, the conversation, the thoughts of a man, indicate what he is. A pure heart is the perfection of humanity. It should be the life-work to cultivate it. It cannot be secured by personal effort alone. Determination, discipline, will, all combined, make only the philosopher, who is far short of the Christian. Prayer is the source of spiritual power. There can be no genuine purity without it. God must be the acknowledged author of it. With all our passion and depravity and weakness, if we only do not delight in them, but wish to be delivered from them, we should go before God in earnest prayer. We should expect to achieve and maintain purity through Christ, and through him alone.

Undoubtedly, as Christ views our hearts, we are all guilty of having broken many, perhaps all of the commandments. Who can forgive past sin? Who can nip sinful passion in the bud? Who can preserve us from sinking in the cold flood of atheism, gloom, and despair? None but Christ. Without Christ it will certainly come to that at last. With his aid we may stand, stand securely, stand forever. "But let him that standeth take heed lest he fall." Heed even the exhortation of earthly wisdom, *Obsta principiis*—Avoid the beginnings of evil. Watch the door of the soul. Let the very heart be an altar consecrated to God.

X.

THE EIGHTH COMMANDMENT.

The Crime of Theft.

THOU SHALT NOT STEAL.—Exodus xx, 15.

Is not this commandment to us entirely superfluous? What child of Christian parents, what man or woman accustomed to enter a Christian house of worship, does not know that it is wrong to steal? Is it not almost an insult to exhort a man not to steal? The apostle, writing to a Church that had lately been converted from heathenism, might with propriety say, "Let him that stole steal no more;" but would it not indicate weakness of judgment and indelicacy of taste, for a preacher now to give such an exhortation to a respectable congregation?

Perhaps so; and yet I shall assume that all honest people would like to have their integrity fortified, and be ready at all times to render a reason for their strict adherence to the law of *meum* and *tuum*. Perhaps some of us are honest simply because we have not been sorely tried. It is not positively certain but that if we could put our hands into the public treasury, or some other large treasury, without danger of detection, the temptation might make our honesty waver! Others, seemingly as strong and as scrupulous as we, have sinned. It cannot harm us to inquire into the reasons for any commandment of God.

Private property must be recognized or industry will be paralyzed, all its wondrous products will vanish; the larger portion of the world's inhabitants will perish from inanition; weeds, forest-trees, and wild beasts will again overspread the earth's surface, and the few human beings that remain will, in the warmer regions of the earth, in nakedness and ignorance, fight for existence with the brutes, and feed miserably on the spontaneous productions of the soil. None but a fanatic can desire that private property should not be recognized and maintained.

Nor would it affect the principle if human beings were organized into phalansteries instead of families. Each phalanstery would then be an individual, to hold its vast or meager estates, for some of them would be poor and starving, others reveling in wealth. There is no way to escape the conclusion: Property must be recognized, or man must be an ignorant animal, scarcely king above brutes.

But it is not wholly, perhaps, nor chiefly, on this account, that the claims to personal property are asserted by the Almighty, and enforced in his commandments. A moral development of man is secured by the recognition of property. Industry, prudence, foresight, study, self-denial, regard for the claims of others, benevolence, are all either originated or largely stimulated and developed by the recognition of property. As well endeavor to grasp the ocean with all it contains in one view of the eye, as to comprehend all the multifarious benefits of recognizing property in one mental conception. The providence of the father, the economy of the mother, the skill of the artisan, the comprehensive power of the master workman, tho grasp of the engineer, the skillful calculations of the merchant and the banker, are all due to the recognition of property. Its effect upon the mind is far more valuable than upon the body.

Again, the acknowledgment of the claims of others, forbearing to trespass upon them, even under violent temptation, makes self-control strong, the will prompt and commanding, and the man worthy to be regarded as possessing a soul suggestive of immortality.

If all this is true, theft must be forbidden and prevented.

Even those who tolerate it must be few and exceptional, and in their own organizations must disavow it. Thieves in the same band are not allowed to steal from each other. Hence the proverb, there is honor among thieves.

The cancer has a kind of life and growth of its own, stealing its nourishment from the surrounding flesh. It is rather a beautiful thing in itself, and only hateful because it does not earn its own living, and tends to destroy the larger and better organism on which it feeds. So bands of robbers and pirates have a government of their own, generally despotic and very rigid, systematic and beautiful often, if only they would earn their own right to live, and not consume the more rightfully claimed substance of the surrounding society.

But may not a valid apology for theft be pleaded from the unequal distribution of property? What marvelous and seemingly unjust distinctions exist among men! One lives in a palace, a model of beautiful architecture, with a cellar well stored, a full library, and abundant works of art, and with all the comforts and luxuries that epicurean taste can suggest. He opens the door and looks out upon his vast hereditary acres; he enters his elegant carriage, and is drawn by beautiful horses for hours through his own lands. Is he ill? the most skillful physicians attend him; servants are ready to anticipate every want and gratify every desire; flatterers and parasites hover around him; his poor thoughts are pronounced amazing wisdom, and his silliest commonplace expressions are received as exquisite wit. He lives a Sybarite, dies in luxury, and is buried in gold, attended by a long train of flatterers, who treat him as though a being of a higher grade than themselves, and a lying epitaph is inscribed on the splendid monument that covers his worthless dust.

By his side, or on the outskirts of his vast and useless estate, there lives a man of a strong intellect and a pure heart, but penury oppressed him from his birth. Doomed to exhaust his energies in excessive physical labor, with mind and body stinted for want of food, confined to the locality that gave him birth, despised by those inferior to him in talent and morals, and superior only in wealth, with wife and children famishing from the small compensation received for his excessive labor, is it wrong for such a man, if he can do it with safety to himself, to purloin some of the property of his plethoric neighbor?

Let it not be thought that arguments may not be pleaded for theft. Very many who have engaged in it have succeeded in convincing themselves that it is right. "I rob the rich and give alms to the poor," has been the motto of more than one highwayman. Even pirates, when putting their victims to death, have been known to make the sign of the cross, and have resented all opposition to their peculiar religious tenets.

All this shows the weakness or the limitations of the human reason. The correctness of conclusions depends not only upon the accuracy of the logical process, but also upon the correctness of the premises assumed. Once allow that it is ever right knavishly or secretly to steal, and it is practically impossible to draw a line anywhere to protect society from disorganization and man from barbarism.

Yet on this, as on all other fundamentals of right, circumstances are conceivable, and may be rarely actual, when one principle of duty seems to come into collision with another, and the man may properly judge for himself which he is to obey. Thus it would be right to take the property of another in order to save life, to save one's self or family from starvation; and though in such a case undiscriminating human law might condemn, the charity of man and the law of God would exonerate from guilt. In such a case a man's right to live would override the claim of his neighbor to property.

That temptations to theft are mightily enhanced by the unjust and perpetuated inequalities in society, especially in the older nations, and under despotic governments, cannot be denied. It is not pleasant to see the palace and hovel side by side, or to hear the hilarious shouts of revelry and the moans of the famishing borne on the same breeze. But these evils are not to be overcome by theft. That, allowed, would indeed destroy the palace and silence the hilarity, but it would not expand the hovel or hush the cry of starvation.

The evils of unjust poverty, growing out of a vicious organization of society, must be attacked by improving the social basis, by repealing unjust laws, annulling old abuses, suppressing monopolies, and by making it possible for men to obtain a just reward for labor and economy. In the mean time laws that exist must be obeyed, while the ax is applied to the roots of old abuses, and more benign and just institutions are cultivated in their place.

Christianity is doing this work constantly, and with irresistible power. The spirit of the Gospel has nearly abolished feudalism, unjust imprisonment, cruel and vengeful punishments for crime or for debt, persecution for opinions; and yet will remove the entailing of estates by primogeniture, and will offer the Sabbath for rest, and the advantages of intelligence and education to all men.

It is noticeable that the old national government of the Israelites, divinely instituted through Moses, had it been thoroughly executed, would have rendered slavery and ignorance and severe poverty nearly impossible. There was never seen among men a constitution, of human origin, so liberal, impartial, and benign as the old Israelitish theocracy. By it all the landed estate of the vast nation was fairly distributed among the families. Every seven years all debts were canceled, all serfdom abolished, and every fifty years the original equality restored. It is true that we have reason to doubt whether this constitution was ever faithfully obeyed; but this failure, like their idolatry, was the fault of the people, and not the design of God. As the sun is brighter than the stars, so the Israelitish constitution, in humanity, liberality, and the recognition of individual rights, surpassed all other governments of antiquity. It shows most clearly the handiwork of God. Whence had Moses that wisdom, that regard for the claims of every man? Had he learned theism from idolatrous Egypt? Had he learned to provide against degradation and poverty from a land whose slaves built the pyramids? Whence did the prophets learn so fiercely to declaim against the oppression of the poor, and to denounce the severest of divine vengeance upon the covetous and proud?

Temptations to theft were never so strong among the Israelites as in modern times; and there can be no doubt that one effectual way to lessen crime is to abolish all artificial and wrong temptations to it.

This crime is one to which poverty and degradation impel their victims. Who can entertain so keen a sense of condemnation toward the slave on the plantation or in the house—who is never legally entitled to any property, and who is forced to toil for his owner from birth till death, according to a compact which he has never consented to—if he embraces every opportunity to plunder his owner's property? Is it wrong for a slave to steal? I will not pronounce it right. I will not say that it would be wholly destitute of wrong. But this I will say, that a slave who should strictly abstain from theft on principle, would exhibit a sublimer virtue than a freman ever could by obedience to this commandment. His obedience would be purely virtuous. He would honor a commandment that could never be directly of any great benefit to him. He has no property that his master may not lawfully steal.

The unjust laws by which the claims of a few landholders are secured in England, in opposition to the deserved demands of the many, directly foster theft. There are more professed thieves in London, alone, than there are landholders in Great Britain; and, unfortunately, the number of landholders is becoming less, and the number of thieves is becoming greater. The law by which landed estates descend to the oldest son, while the younger sons and all the daughters receive only what the parents are able to provide, which is sometimes much and sometimes nothing, has no foundation in right reason or the nature of things. It leads to terrible abuses. God is not the author of the poverty and degradation among men. The Irish famine, which swept away thousands, was not an executor of divine vengeance, except to indicate the consequence of misgovernment and whisky drinking. The doctrine of Malthus, that the world is, always was, and always must be overcrowded with population, so that want and suffering are inevitable, is a libel upon the Creator, and not sustained by facts.

Now, under the influence of Christianity, the constant tendency of institutions is toward improvement. All writers and speakers who can reach the hearts of the people and command their attention are in favor of improvement. Every new law is better than the one which it displaced. Happy is that nation that can thus revolutionize abuses and wrongs gradually and without bloodshed. But if the abuse assumes to govern and to spread, and will not go down except by violence, then Christianity itself will nerve the heart and arm the warrior who fights for justice and humanity.

The time for the toleration of organic and perpetual violations of the law of right is passing away; and wherever the New Testament with the Old is read, warm discussion and earnest declamation against wrong will exist, and ere long unjust institutions will, peacefully or violently, fall to the ground.

Theft is, probably, a greater sin in the United States of America than in any other part of the world, simply because the temptations to it are so slight. The land teems with abundance. Hunger is a disagreeable feeling which not one in ten thousand of its people ever really felt. Another nation could be fed with what its people waste. The blessings of education and culture are placed within the reach of all. The distinctions in society are the least perhaps compatible with that energy and ambition requisite to impel a people to profitable industry.

And yet I doubt whether we can claim to be a peculiarly honest people. Crimes against property are alarmingly numerous. Our state prisons, houses of correction, and other punitive institutions are numerous, and never empty. A steady army march into them, and when released for the most part return, and seldom rise to respectable, honorable life. And though the greater part of these unhappy offenders come from the miserable population that hang around our grog-shops and saloons in the large cities, the children of degraded people that the nations of Europe vomit upon our shores, yet there are not wanting some from our own well-educated families who find their way through the same avenues to the same end.

And not a few others, who, tempted by the cheap luxuries offered in our land of plenty, seek to obtain them by gambling, or forgery, or counterfeiting money, or other forms of theft. The number of such persons in a single neighborhood may not be large, but in the aggregate it would astonish all who reflect upon it.

But these are not the most common forms of theft. There are forms of it common even among us.

The first and most common form is perhaps idleness. What is an habitually idle man but a thief? The apostle's requirement is, "If a man will not work neither let him eat." Every man owes to the world and to God the results of a vigorous, active, honorable life. Withholding that, he does not pay his debts. Idleness, itself a crime, for which a well-instructed conscience will promptly condemn a man, is also the prolific source of other crimes. Seldom does an idle man become a Christian; and never without at once throwing off his habits of idleness.

Every kind of fraud in business is a violation of the eighth commandment.

Well may this kind of demon say, "Our name is legion, for we are many." Who shall describe the tricks of manufacture and of trade, by which unsound articles are represented as good, and every imaginable object that passes through the hands of one man to another is made the means of unjust gain? Even our food and medicines are adulterated; poison is sold for food; and the sick man is cheated at once out of his money and his life by the knavish dealer.

It is lamentable that so low a tone of public opinion on this subject prevails almost universally. Traders defend each other because it is common, and the people consent to be wronged, or rely more upon their own shrewdness than upon the honesty of others. Too often when detected, the very art of the thief is pleaded as a kind of extenuation for the crime.

Far be it from me to charge all men of business with a violation of this commandment. On the other hand, their regard for its sacredness in many respects is sublime. The confidence of business men in each other; the regularity and ease with which the vast transactions of domestic and foreign commerce are accomplished, depending more upon the faith of man in man than upon the power of the law, is sublime; still, it cannot be denied that, through fierce emulation and a feverish anxiety to become rich, the standard of duty adopted by many traders does not correspond with the strict standard of right, and so far it is a violation of the commandment, Thou shalt not steal.

Too many regard it as lawful prey to cheat the poor. The dependent sewing girl is doomed to devote all her waking hours, in many of our large cities, to assiduous wasting toil, wearing out her life for a scanty subsistence, and the very garments the people wear are the price of blood. There is no need of such sacrifice. The world is no richer nor better for it. There are no more garments to wear, and the rich even enjoy no more luxuries. It is only the fierce competition of the manufacturer, who wishes to outdo his neighbor in profit. He should deal justly, and if he cannot support himself by justice leave the business, and expose its wickedness to others. Better die than live by crime.

There is, too, no standard of right, in our treatment of a nation, different from that by which we are governed toward individuals. It is as wrong to defraud the post-office as to defraud our neighbor. It is a crime to lie to the revenue-collector as certainly as it would be to lie to a brother or sister. Church members may sell shoddy cloth for the genuine to the government, but, though their names are on the Church record, they will be on the wrong side of the great account book kept in heaven.

God will hold all amenable to the commandment, Thou shalt not steal.

They that make haste to be rich shall not be innocent. No people need to reflect upon this divine truth more than Americans. It is, perhaps, our sorest temptation, and, next to intemperance in the use of intoxicating drinks, our most prolific source of crime. Riches is too much the badge of honor among us, and stimulates many to an unholy ambition. It becomes all good men to exert their influence in behalf of a higher and holier standard of morality. Strict morality, intellectual ability, unaffected piety, and a contented disposition, with a devotion to the public welfare, should be regarded as the essentials of the highest honor. Mere wealth should be regarded as an adventitious distinction, not conveying an honor unless it has been rightly attained and is properly employed. Whoever exerts his influence in favor of this standard is doing what he can to lessen the temptations toward theft.

Still other forms of violating this commandment might be mentioned, prominent among which are contracting debts without a moral certainty of being able to pay, and obtaining the property of others by gambling.

Both of these practices seem to be somewhat relieved from a direct intention of obtaining the property of others by fraud, since in the case of debt the creditor consents to the obligation, and in the case of gambling the loser consents to the risk. Both practices are wrong. A debt is an appeal to the creditor's trust in your honesty, and to violate the trust so far tends to lower the standard of character among men, besides wronging the creditor. It is to throw one's influence on the side of depravity. It is an injury to the community as well as to the party wronged. Hence debts of honor are considered doubly binding by all men of high moral sense; and all debts should be regarded as debts of honor, except those for which ample security is given when the obligation is assumed.

Gambling is a practice which the native unsophisticated conscience does not pronounce to be wrong. In its beginnings it may not be regarded essentially an evil. But long experience has proved that it appeals to a passion liable to be developed into a mania, and therefore when indulged it invariably produces great evils. Therefore, applying Christ's rule, "By their fruits shall ye know them," a sound morality must condemn it. The easiest way to avoid excess, and to prevent fostering an evil passion in others, is to abstain entirely from the practice. Therefore Christian moralists forbid it. Many a man has been robbed of all his property by games of chance. It is almost invariably connected with fraud. Drunkenness and profanity are almost invariably associated with it. It was never a benefit to any one; it has ruined thousands.

It is no compliment to the Christianity of our country and times, that even religious societies have resorted to it to some extent in their "fairs" and other benevolent meetings, to wring money out of the unwilling, excusing themselves by the poor apology that the proceeds are to be devoted to a good purpose. It is never right to do evil that good may come. If the Church inaugurates and encourages gambling for the cause of God, her ministers and members must not be surprised if others gamble for their own gratification. Nor when the first steps are taken can any logical limit to the practice be laid down. Therefore it is safe to reject it altogether, as forbidden by the eighth commandment.

Our conclusion, then, is, that a strict obedience to this commandment requires that none should assert a claim to property except it be the product of his own skill or labor, or belongs to him by inheritance, gift, or discovery; and that the rightful claims of others should always be acknowledged. This is but the foundation of society; but the responsibilities of property are many and far-reaching, and are more clearly and fully explained in the Gospel.

XI.

THE NINTH COMMANDMENT.

The Value of Truth.

THOU SHALT NOT BEAR FALSE WITNESS AGAINST THY NEIGHBOR.
Exodus xx, 16.

IF there is any faith in which wise men agree, it is that all men should love, promote, and obey truth, and should hate, repel, and destroy falsehood. This great principle is divinely announced in the ninth commandment of the Decalogue.

In elucidating this proposition let us inquire:

I. What is truth, and what is falsehood?

II. Why should we love the one and hate the other.

III. How can these objects be best secured?

I. Truth, in the sense in which we employ the term, implies enunciation, or some form of representation. This implies existences, material or mental, to be announced, declared, or represented.

The essence of truth is, that the representation should exactly correspond with the thing, presenting it to the mind of a person as the thing actually is.

Truths are infinite in number, infinite in variety, infinite in extent; and therefore the realm of truth is boundless, and no single finite mind can comprehend it all. What he cannot comprehend is either altogether unknown or dimly seen, and he either has no opinion about it, or he is not certain whether his notions of it are true or false; and if he has any firm belief in it, it is either unreasonable, and likely to be wrong, or it is based on the information of some other being, whom he thinks it best to trust.

The realm of absolutely known truth to any man is, when compared with the infinite ocean of existence around him, small, though the truths known by some men are much more numerous and extensive than those known by others.

The thing, material or mental, must, of course, exist before it is announced, and often the word truth is used to denote the idea of any existence without reference to any representation of it. Thus we say the philosopher investigates *truth*. The theologian wishes to enforce *truth*.

> "*Truth* crushed to earth will rise again;
> The eternal years of God are hers;
> But error, wounded, writhes in pain,
> And dies amid her worshipers.

Truth, then, strictly speaking, has two meanings, to wit: the correct understanding of a thing, and the correct representation of it to another.

Falsehood, the opposite of truth, may mean either an incorrect, a totally wrong understanding of a thing, or the wrong representation of a thing to another.

The whole universe is a combination of facts. There are certain facts of geography, for instance. The earth on which we stand occupies a certain amount of space, has a certain form and weight and texture; so much of it is covered with water, so much with forests, so much with deserts, so much with snow. Was there ever a man who understood all the facts about the entire surface of the earth, so that if a blank globe was given to him of the same size, and he had the requisite power, he could reproduce exactly everything that is now found on this earth? Not one! Even a Humboldt or a Ritter would only make a few scratches, or draw some outline maps on the globe. Probably not all living men together could complete the picture. And yet some men know much, the most of men a little, of geography. But extend your vision to other worlds, and how little we know. We can count the planets of this solar system—perhaps not all of them. Combined astronomical science might succeed in placing every one in its proper orbit, and set it whirling and advancing at the proper rates, and tell its weight and size, and something about its material, learned lately from the spectroscope; and that is about all. But are they clothed with vegetation? None can reply. Are they inhabited? Possibly; some of them probably; perhaps none. Who knows? We could ask questions by the hour, but no one can satisfactorily answer. This is but one pathway in material things from the little circle which we do understand into the infinite around us. There are innumerable pathways of the kind, just as you can conceive of innumerable radii from a center toward the circumference.

Turn now to mental things. What is thought? What is soul? What is a thinking being? Does a thinking being always carry with it some of those phenomena that we call material? In other words, Is there ever a soul without a body? Who knows?

We know that there are minds. We know that we are minds. We can reason. We can count, measure, combine numbers, and compare qualities, and study angles and curves, until we are lost, and can possibly see no further, and yet are conscious that what we see is no more all than what we know of astronomy is all. We have a dim picture of the past, written in a few books, representing the partial, prejudiced, and fragmentary glimpses of several centuries, giving us not nearly so correct and full a view as a man would get of a landscape from an old blurred photograph taken in a dark day; for much of what we do see is false. And then when we turn our gaze forward in time, and toward that great ocean of eternity which is to come, how little we know of it!

All this shows the very limited amount of truth that man can possibly learn. Indeed, the tendency just now is to discard everything except what may be called ascertained facts. "The Positive Philosophy" is now most ably advocated. The imagination is not to be indulged; faith is not to be recognized; a man is not only to believe only just what he knows from actual sight, but to discard all other thoughts as puerile, or belonging to that age of each man and that age of the world which every wise man and the world ought to outgrow! The senses are to be credited, the intuitions to be denied, forsooth!

This is a silly theory, but it is not my business now to expose its folly. It has often been manifested by obstinate, ignorant persons before it was reduced to the form of philosophy, falsely so called. A truly wise man ought to remember that a human soul never outgrows any of its faculties. Polywogs shed their tails and become frogs, but human beings should never shed their imagination nor their faith. They may develop them, chasten them, and bring them under the proper dominion of reason; but drop them, never. "Positive science" never did fill the whole orb of a man's soul, and never will. Child-like fancy may be developed into a philosophic preconception, which always precedes a scientific discovery, and after the last discovery it still exists. It may also develop into Christian faith that precedes an experience that prepares the soul for heaven.

But if the vision of man at best is so limited, how important is it that what he does know, or what he thinks he knows, should be correct? For who is not aware that many of the beliefs of men are false?

Even many geographic beliefs are false. The most of human beings that have lived have believed that the sun moved around the earth. The most of men now believe it, if they ever think anything about it. Millions think the sun and moon are being swallowed by a huge serpent when eclipsed. Many believe now in lucky and unlucky days, and that what they call changes in the moon change the weather on earth, though, probably, the moon never changed any more in any one minute than in any other minute since it was made! What strange notions the ancients entertained about the ocean, the air, fire, and earth, the precious metals, the philosopher's stone, and the influence of the stars? How many baseless notions are now entertained?

What groundless prejudices exist among the people of different nations toward each other! Not many years ago it was a part of the education of the Englishman and the Frenchman to hate each other. How many cruelties have been justified by a misinterpretation of the biblical expression, "Cursed be Canaan, a servant of servants shall he be!"

II. But why is truth preferable to falsehood? Is it universally conceded to be so? Is not a pleasing delusion better than a disagreeable fact? I have heard this doctrine maintained. It has even been said by divines, in their defense of the Christian religion, that were it not true, so pleasing is the doctrine of the love of Christ, so elevating to man is a belief in the immortality of the soul, so productive of the best interests of society are the practical teachings of the Gospel, they would still defend it. I do not sympathize with that position. I would say, Let me have *the truth*, though it be bitter, rather than error, though it be sweet. I do not envy the lunatic his visions, though they make him laugh. If the temple I am building is only a cob-house or a palace of straw, let me know it, though all my hopes are dashed to the ground. I would rather die at once with truth than live any length of time with error.

In this thought, too, I am but expressing a common passion of healthy thinking souls.

Truth, then, is to be coveted, loved, uttered, and maintained, *because God has made man to love it.* It is enough that truth is intuitively desirable, falsehood intuitively disagreeable.

Now this love of truth is not depravity. It is the healthy, right exercise of our intellect. It is the one right stimulant of the mind. Love of error is a perversion. That is depravity. God loves truth. He has so declared. A little thought will convince any one that it must be so. The very idea of God supposes a being who *cannot be deceived.* It is impossible for God to imagine a falsehood without knowing it to be a falsehood. He sees things as they are. If there be in things the relations of time—past, present, and future, God knows things properly —the past as past, the present as present, and the future as future. If the future in any of its parts actually now exists as undetermined and contingent, then God knows it as such, and to know it in any other condition would be to know a falsehood, of which he is incapable. If things exist in relation to space, as material things seem to us to exist, and as immaterial souls may or may not exist, (we cannot ascertain,) God sees them as they are, and cannot be deceived; and when we come to see as we are seen and know as we are known, we shall not be deceived.

Therefore, for a man to say that he would prefer falsehood to truth because the falsehood may be pleasing, is deliberately to choose to be unlike God; it is, consequently, the cardinal sin, and such a choice betrays already a radical depravity.

It is the prime characteristic of a healthy mind, that it longs to know the truth; it longs, too, that all its knowings shall be true. It detests false cognitions, spurious faiths, delusive opinions. It has no objection to imaginations, if they are only perceived to be imaginations; it likes the dreams of a poet in the place of dreams, but not as facts.

Another reason for the love of truth is a profound conviction that in the end truth is the only safe guide. Though falsehoods may delude and please for a season, all who believe in such a God as the Bible describes, himself truthful and just and holy, must see that the end of all false beliefs is evil, just in proportion to the degree of their falsity; and all true faiths are valuable in proportion to the degree of their trueness.

It takes ideas a long time to produce their legitimate fruits; but if God has written any lesson indelibly upon all his works, in every possible character it is that truth begets perfection and error begets deformity; truth begets joy, error begets pain; truth leads to life, error leads to death.

This may be predicated, so far as its influence

extends, of every individual truth and of every individual error. Every lie on any subject, however abstruse, or impractical, or trivial, if believed, is dangerous. Every truth, however trivial, may prove to have a value. We can conceive of instances in which lies may seem temporarily to benefit men, just as we can conceive of instances in which poisons may be of benefit to the body, or wounds or bruises may help a man; but they are exceptional, and do not affect the rule: all error is pernicious; all truth is profitable.

Truth, on any one subject, obeyed, will bear its legitimate fruit, though the same mind that entertains it is a victim of error on other subjects. The temperate sinner will be healthy, as the fruit of his temperance; the intemperate saint will be sickly, as the fruit of his intemperance. But the temperate sinner will suffer in his soul as the result of his sins, while the intemperate saint will be profited spiritually by his mental rectitude. But generally error begets error of other kinds, and truth encourages truth of every other kind. All errors, though mutually contradictory and hostile, agree in a combined hostility to truth; while any one truth correctly ascertained predisposes the mind for other truths. Therefore science must aid religion, and religion must aid science. Any science, so called, that is hostile to true religion, is sophistical and false; and any religion that is hostile to true science is superstitious and wrong.

A truly religious man is always ready to acknowledge and investigate any fact. He does not shrink from facts of history, however they may seem to bear upon the Bible, or from facts of science, however they may seem to conflict with theology. He is ready at any time to adjust his notions to facts, without sacrificing what he regards as central actual virtues. The man who is not wiser to-day than he was yesterday is not a model man. The theology of to-day is not the same in form as that of a century ago. The past cannot be restored without its ignorance, and who would desire that?

Some men have no faith in truth, as able to defend itself. They make a cage and put truth in it, and bandage its eyes, and clip its wings, and then say to all around, Come and see how much we love truth! Do you love it? then break down the bars, tear off the bandages, and let the captive fly. If it be a creature of God he will take care of it.

Some have maintained that all fiction is to be discarded by carrying out the principle of this commandment.

This is a narrow view and false. God has given us imagination to be indulged. We need it, to picture before us by anticipation the results of wrong action, to repel us from it; and of right action, to attract us to it. Hypotheses always precede scientific deductions and intelligent inventions. The wildest of fancies may be useful. They may even illustrate the highest truth. It is only needful that they should be known as fictions, and not regarded as true.

The deliberate falsifier is perhaps the greatest of sinners. He perverts the intellect, which is the fountain of action, to falsify and corrupt the very nature of those over whom he exerts an influence. The devil is called in the Scripture "the father of lies," and is pronounced "a liar from the beginning." It must have been a lie, deliberately chosen and defended, that caused the fallen angels to swerve from the integrity in which God first created them. Falsehood has been and is the source of all sin.

"But there are instances of lies recorded in the Bible, and attributed even to men and women that were commended, if not for their falsehoods, certainly for their general character." Certainly there are. Such as Jacob, who deceived Isaac by the help of his good mother; and Rahab, who concealed the spies and lied to her own countrymen, on the principle that all is right in war, and was afterward commended as a woman of faith; and David, who feigned madness to save his life. What shall we say of them? Simply this. The Bible described facts as they occurred, and not the fancies of its writers. Also these people, so far as they sinned, could not have been approved by a just God, and it would have been better had they not borne false witness, though it was *not against* their neighbor, except in the case of Jacob, who was undoubtedly punished for his sin, and was in no way benefited by the birthright which he stole.

In the clearer revelations of the Old Testament we are told to adhere to the truth. Liars as well as their lies are to be destroyed.

It seems now like descending to small particulars, to insist that a man should never bear false witness against his neighbor. Whoever does this commits two sins, a sin against truth and a sin against his neighbor. Living as we do in Christian light, and with our modern culture, we may follow the example of Jesus, and even strengthen the commandment, and say, Thou shalt not bear false witness either against or for thy neighbor. "Lie not at all." Bear no false witness; not even to do good. "There be some who say of us that we do evil that good may come." And what did the apostle say to those who thus slandered him and his brethren? "Whose damnation is just." The apostle would not have lied to convert the whole Roman empire to Christianity. If he would have done it, I should reject him as a teacher inspired by the Spirit of God. Were there one single instance of a falsehood recorded against Jesus, I should reject him as the Son of God, or the prophet whom we ought to believe.

To enumerate all the methods of bearing false witness against our neighbor is impossible, but perhaps some of the most common classes of this witness may be mentioned.

Whenever selfishness leads a man to magnify his own claims and unjustly to depreciate those of his neighbor, he breaks this commandment. Whenever envy leads us to withhold deserved approbation from the good traits of another, we break this commandment. That trait of character which delights in evil-speaking, in merciless criticism, in slander, and exults over the disgrace of another, springs from a love of falsehood. Falsehood is the precise opposite of that charity which "thinketh no evil," and "covers" or conceals "a multitude of sins;" not from a love of the sins, but from a conviction that an exposure of them is not demanded, and would do no good.

How many histories, so called, are tissues of lies! How many political essays, and even religious writings, so called, are permeated with falsehood! How disgraceful to Christianity is the word, how much more disgraceful the thing expressed by the word, "pious frauds!" Is there any reproach to our fallen human nature so deep as the fact that the very word derived from the name of Jesus, the Son of God, *jesuitism*, signifies chicanery and lies? Is not this indeed "stealing the livery of heaven to serve the devil in?"

The very air we breathe in this world seems to be filled with the poison of falsehood. As a destructive gas in some miasmatic atmosphere is inhaled in every breath, so it seems impossible to escape this universal contagion. Nor does it die out, but seems to grow with what it feeds upon. In compliments, insincerity; in politeness, flattery; in reproof, envy; in love and hatred, prejudice; even in religious investigation, party spirit and an unjust fear of the pure truth, compel us all always to stand on guard, lest we be misled and deceived by the omnipresent pressure of falsehood.

It is said that children always believe all that is told them. That may be so at first, but they soon learn by bitter experience to be suspicious and faithless; and the first sin that most children commit is to tell a lie.

III. Without attempting to specify the innumerable methods of breaking this commandment, let us briefly notice how the evil may be most successfully attacked. Some of the most efficient remedies are the following:

1. Consider first the prime characteristic of God—truth.

There is not a thing in nature primarily designed to deceive. We speak fancifully of the deceitful ocean, the deceitful mirage of the desert, of poisonous fruits and flowers attracting us by their beauty only to injure and destroy. But all these things exist according to law, inflexible, unchanging. They do not change their natures and their shapes. The instincts of the unreasoning animals are always a sure guide, and if man will use his reason he may learn the facts and laws of nature, which abide. "The Father of Lights" has "no changeableness or shadow of turning." What is this but to say that he is *true?* The laws of nature, never varying, are the sublimest expression of truth.

2. Reflect, secondly, upon Christ. Read his life over and over again, and see how absolutely free from the least tinge of falsehood it is. We have no intimations that he was suspected even of this sin. Paul was charged with the fault. Peter actually did dissemble, and was rebuked by Paul for the wrong; but the Saviour not only always uttered the truth, and nothing but the truth, but was never suspected of the opposite. His words were sometimes perverted, even when he knew it and did not correct the wrong impressions; but he was never responsible for an incorrect idea. He was "the Way, THE TRUTH, the Life."

3. Observe, thirdly, that a deliberate untruth always annihilates that peculiar peace which is the greatest reward of a Christian life. It is an essential element of Christian doctrine that every true spiritual disciple of Christ who has repented, believed, and become a child of God by adoption, has a peace that no other possession will give, and that nothing but sin can permanently take away. This peace abides till death. It flows as a river. It destroys the fear of death. It illumines the grave. It ushers the departing soul into heaven. Now there is no more deadly foe to this Christian peace than a conscious falsehood. It is an unfailing poison, a deadly enemy.

It was this that prevented the early Christians, when threatened with martyrdom, from saving their lives by an insincere compliance with the ceremonies of paganism. Many a Christian was told that if he would but offer a sacrifice to an idol, if he would but toss a piece of incense upon the altar, if he would but disown Christ by a word, though he might still cherish him in his heart, he should be unmolested. Why did he not yield so little? Was it not obstinacy? So it seemed to many. But their reply was in substance: "I cannot do this small thing without sanctioning what I believe to be a lie. Truth is to me a precious thing. If I pervert it my peace of mind is gone. My conscious hold upon my unseen Redeemer broken. I am cast off, a waif, an orphan, helpless, dead. I live only by preserving my integrity. I can bear martyrdom, which can last but a few moments. I cannot bear desolation which may be eternal;" and therefore the Christian died. But so sublime was the example, that appealing to the natural admiration of sincerity in every heart, for one that fell two arose to take his place, and "the blood of the martyrs was the seed of the Church."

Emulate this example, and preserve your Christian peace by adhering to the truth.

4. If it be proper to add a feebler motive after the strongest ones, notice, fourthly, that a reputation for truthfulness is one of the most solid and substantial sources of strength and success that a man can have. "There is a man whose word is as good as his bond," is a testimony that money cannot estimate for a business man. "There is a speaker or writer who weighs well what he says, and never speaks hastily or extravagantly," leads you involuntarily to offer him a tribute of admiration. The fact is, men do naturally feel some sort of reverence for God; and the man of truth is so far like God.

But, remember that a reputation cannot, as a general thing, be obtained, and certainly not long maintained, unless it has a solid foundation to rest upon. To have this solid strength of reputation we must have the character on which the superstructure is built.

There are national characteristics and characteristics of certain ages. Whole peoples, whether justly or otherwise, have had the reputation of deceivers. The classic reader is familiar with the term "Punic faith;" and, in modern times, the reputation of the Chinese in business matters, and of some leading European nations in social matters, is not enviable. Much more honorable was the reputation of the Romans for integrity. If the old stories of Regulus and Cincinnatus were fabulous, still a people that could delight in such fables revered truth. But especially where Christianity is preached in its purity, where the people read for themselves the Bible, we have a right to expect that strong virtue whose central support is truth.

Finally, let no one suppose that it is an easy thing to abstain from falsehood and always to abide by the truth. It is the very summit of manhood. It is emancipation from sin; it is union with God.

It has, therefore, its counterfeits.

The true man is not necessarily disagreeable. He is not necessarily uttering his opinions obtrusively, and out of time and place, where they cannot be understood or effective of good. He is not required to be dogmatic, or to suppose that his opinions, though he believes them, are necessarily correct, or that others who differ from him are necessarily insincere. There is a unity of intention and purpose more valuable than a unity of opinion. The man of genuine faith and sincerity will respect those qualities in others though they differ from him. Education and circumstances must and will affect belief.

The man of truth is not required always to be sober and sedate, or to abstain even from giving utterance to hypotheses, and fancies, and fables, and even falsehoods, if he does not intend that they shall be believed, but is simply exercising, in a legitimate way, the imagination or the wit with which his Maker endowed him. No one blames John Bunyan for writing his Pilgrim's Progress so artistically that many a child while reading it has believed it to be literally true. Few censure Defoe for writing Robinson Crusoe with such a verisimilitude that almost every one has once believed it; or his account of the London Plague so skillfully, that but for the positive knowledge that it is a lie all would believe it. Divines are even divided in opinion about some of the narratives in the New Testament, as to whether they are parables or literally true, and neither hypothesis interferes with the substantial moral truth which they are designed to illustrate. How does it affect the religious instruction to be conveyed by the book of Job, or the book of Jonah, whether we consider the one as a poem and the other as an allegory?

And yet this caution is to be observed: that men who are gifted with a fertile inventive fancy should not palm off as history the creations of their own brains.

The most pernicious example of this is, perhaps, the silly novel written fifty years ago by one Solomon Spalding, a minister of the Gospel, in a kind of scriptural style, which was afterward appropriated by the notorious Joe Smith as a sacred book that he pretended to have received from an angel, and has been made the foundation of the faith of that ignorant and corrupt people called the Mormons. History does not describe another so glaring an instance of the pernicious consequences of believing a lie, which was never intended by its author to be received as anything but the product of his fancy. And yet it is doubtful whether the author of the novel can be held responsible for the stupidity and fanaticism of the people who seized upon the creation of his fancy and made it a god.

We should also be encouraged by the belief that, in the end, truth alone will triumph. Error is essentially changeable and mortal. It is protean in its shapes, and can survive only by constantly assuming new forms. Every refuge of lies shall be destroyed. Truth alone is eternal. Institutions based on partial truth may rise rapidly and have a wonderful growth, and promise to be universal, but their defect soon proves fatal. But the central principles of religion abide. All forms of idolatry, being radically wrong, must pass away. Slavery, ignorance, fanaticism, despotism, contradicting essential principles of truth, must disappear. A belief in God, in immortality, in the intrinsic value of virtue and hatefulness of vice, in the revelation of God in Jesus Christ and in his Church, in the efficacy of repentance and faith and spiritual communion with God through prayer and obedience, are essentially true and must abide. Therefore Christianity, being as old as creation and as permanent as God, has nothing to fear. Its defenders should never fear. It is founded on a rock, and all its children are sustained by an unchanging Father; and though the heavens and earth be destroyed God shall abide, and his children shall never perish.

XII.

THE TENTH COMMANDMENT.

Coveting the Goods of Other Men.

THOU SHALT NOT COVET THY NEIGHBOR'S HOUSE, THOU SHALT NOT COVET THY NEIGHBOR'S WIFE, NOR HIS MAN-SERVANT, NOR HIS MAID-SERVANT, NOR HIS OX, NOR HIS ASS, NOR ANY THING THAT IS THY NEIGHBOR'S.—Exodus xx, 17.

THE drapery in which this commandment is clothed is suited to the capacity and habits of thinking of the people who first heard it; the commandment itself is sublime, universally binding, and every way worthy of its claim to divine origin. Had the commandment been addressed to us primarily, it might have been expressed in some such way as this: "Thou shalt not covet thy neighbor's property, nor reputation, nor domestic prosperity, nor bodily strength, nor genius, nor popularity, nor high station, nor anything that is thy neighbor's." The principle of the two phraseologies is the same.

It is true of all the Bible, that it has a style of language, illustration, and to some extent even of argument, growing out of the mental constitution and education and habits of the persons selected to write it, and also of those who were first to hear it. On this account errors in rhetoric, science, or even logic, if any such there are, do not invalidate its authority. What we are to look at is the sptrit, the obvious intent, of the communication made. When God chose human language as an instrument of conveying thought and feeling, he chose an imperfect instrument. Its results cannot be complete. Honest minds, even, do not and cannot receive the same thoughts from it. What language expresses depends as much upon the capacity and character of the receiver as upon those of the speaker. Sometimes the hearer understands more and sometimes less than, and often something very different from, what the speaker intended. But God has not only used this imperfect medium, language, but also habits, natural phenomena, modes of thinking and feeling and acting of certain ages, which are constantly changing, some of which are obsolete, and cannot be thoroughly understood. Hence there is a Bible in the Bible, which it should be the object of preachers to investigate and publish.

From this we may see the importance of a cultivated, honest, and pious ministry; for without culture, honesty, and piety, no one is competent to explain the Bible. From this also we should learn the lesson of charity toward those who differ from us in the explanation of parts of sacred writ, and not be censorious toward any who manifest a regard for God's honor and man's welfare, though their views of the Holy Writings may be different from those which we are taught to entertain.

The principal of the last commandment of the ten is, that no man should covet what properly belongs to another.

There is a kind of coveting which is not wrong. Paul instructed the people to "covet earnestly the best gifts." And again he says, "Covet to prophesy." Coveting in this case means simply to desire strongly.

But coveting, or, as it is generally termed, covetousness, is severely denounced in the Bible. It seems generally to mean something like avarice: an insatiable desire to get and hold and hoard, irrespective of the convenience and comfort of others, and not with a generous purpose to use property to bless man, and honor its author, God. It is pronounced a cardinal sin, and one of "the fruits of the flesh," in opposition to spiritual excellence, and as directly hostile to eternal life.

It is worthy of notice that all sin is either a deficiency or an excess of something which in its proper degree is good. Thus, eating is proper, gluttony is a sin; anger is proper sometimes, malice is always a sin; rest is often proper, idleness a sin; care is proper, a restless, fretting anxiety is a sin. So equally the want of indignation at wrong, the want of proper rest, the want of a proper industry, is a sin. Virtue or right occupies the medium place; on either side is sin.

Our text does not forbid the desiring of a house, or of a wife or husband, or of a man-servant or maid-servant; or, to use terms more consonant with our modes of thinking, it does not forbid us to desire health, wealth, honor, influence, success, or prosperity. It does not forbid us to desire scholarship, or talent, or skill, or eloquence, or any other good thing. What would life be without desire? A juiceless thing, an empty shell. Desire nerves the soul, stimulates the intellect, moves the man. Desire makes the scholar. As the wise man saith, "Through desire, a man having separated himself, seeketh and intermeddleth with all wisdom." Desire creates wealth and spends it. Desire impels the missionary to preach, and the messenger of mercy to carry aid to the dying. Our Saviour was intensely moved by desire when he said, "I *must* work." Desire to accomplish his purpose was his only necessity.

But there is a kind of desiring which is wrong. If we desire to obtain what belongs to another without paying for it, and making it properly our own, we violate the command, "Thou shalt not covet."

This coveting is wrong, for the only object of

desire is to lead to action, and the desire takes its moral character from the kind of action which it tends to produce; but this desire tends to produce only wrong action.

Coveting what belongs to another, if it ripens into action, produces theft. Coveting what belongs to our neighbor is also wrong, even if it does not ripen into action, from its pernicious influence on the soul that indulges in it. It is an unhappy, fretting, gnawing passion. It tends to develop into envy, which differs from coveting our neighbor's possessions only in the natural addition of hatred toward our neighbor, simply because he possesses what we have not. This is, perhaps, the meanest passion of a depraved heart. It is one often felt, seldom acknowledged. It is exhibited in the countenance, in action, but is never confessed.

It is seen in the detraction of others eminent for any excellence. A man who indulges in this passion is ready to undervalue and decry others who belong to the same class with himself. Is he a merchant, his neighbor in the trade is fraudulent, sells for enormous profits, has inferior goods, prospers by arts best known to himself, such as honest dealers would scorn to employ! Is he a physician, his rival is ignorant, rash, unsafe, a charlatan! Is he a lawyer, his brother in the profession, though somewhat successful, is really an inferior man, and succeeds more by show than by merit, and will soon fall down to his level! Is he a minister—for even ministers are liable to like passions with other men—his brethren who seem to surpass him in some kind of success, owe it altogether to a showy or superficial talent, and only illustrate the stupidity of the people rather than any merit of their own! And thus we might pass through the whole catalogue of occupations and positions in society. Coveting what is our neighbor's, and envying the prosperity of our neighbor, are a poison striving to force itself into every depraved heart, and showing itself in a thousand protean shapes. It breeds discontentment, murmuring at Providence, sourness of disposition, fretfulness, ingratitude, and spiritual death.

The wise man in his book of Proverbs very emphatically and beautifully expresses a fact, when he says, "Envy slayeth the silly one." No passion is so universally pernicious to one who indulges it. It paralyzes ambition; it unfits a man to enjoy even the good he possesses. It turns his own sweet to sour, his own prosperity to defeat. The man who envies those whom he regards as more prosperous than himself, distrusts those whom he regards as less prosperous, because he is conscious that he deserves or probably receives their hatred. It is, therefore, a hellish passion, diametrically opposed to the reigning passion of heaven, which is love.

No man will defend this passion; no man desires to cherish it; all men are tempted to indulge it. We shall therefore find it practically profitable to examine its causes and its remedy.

The most fruitful occasion of envy is the strange difference which exists in the bodily and mental condition of men, and apparently in the rewards and penalties of society. This fact has troubled careful thinkers, and especially moralists, of all ages and countries. Some are born with vigorous bodily constitutions, and in spite of recklessness and intemperance live to old age with little pain; others begin to breathe with physical discomfort, subsist with difficulty, and pass through indescribable physical agony. Some have a flow of animal spirits tending always to boisterous merriment and unmeaning laughter; others seem to have been stamped with melancholy from their birth. Some seem to be clothed mentally and morally with the hide of a rhinoceros, and are incapable of taking or intentionally giving an offense; others are as sensitive as an æolian harp, singing with joy, or wailing in pain, as the fitful breezes happen to blow.

Now when men become painfully self-conscious of what they regard as a peculiarity, or an infirmity, it makes them unhappy, and they inquire, Why are others more highly favored than I? Then, if the mind is not rightly directed, it is easy to step into coveting what belongs to the neighbor, and to envy.

This tendency is heightened by the unjust distinctions of society. The world seems fully as partial as the great Author of our being in the bestowment of benefits. Some men toil with the muscle, some men toil with the brain, from ten to twenty hours a day, simply to procure subsistence; others rust away in self-indulgence and ease; others still choose just the amount and variety of labor which they think best. Moreover, each one is inclined to undervalue his own comforts and honors, and overestimate his neighbor's. This fact is very beautifully described by the Roman satirist, who represents the merchant as envying the soldier, and the maimed soldier as envying the merchant; the lawyer as coveting the quiet plenty of the farmer, and the weary farmer as envying the ease and honor of the lawyer.* This fact is palpable to ordinary observation.

I have said above that God is the author of some of these distinctions. I do not wish thereby to throw upon the Almighty a charge which he does not acknowledge, nor in this hasty generalization to omit an examination of special

* Horace, Satire I.

and secondary causes; and least of all to excuse any injustice of society in enslaving or oppressing the poor. I doubt not many wrongs can be righted, many abuses abolished, and many inequalities removed. But while they do exist God permits them, and they are distributed without reference to moral character. Some of them are the results of the sins of others, and befall the innocent. Thus God allows, and, as things are, approves of these inequalities.

Different kinds, and different degrees in the same kind of excellence, are needful to stimulate ambition and industry. The man who feels his deficiency should not envy his more fortunate neighbor, but endeavor to overtake him in the road to merit or enjoyment, and if he cannot surpass him in one pursuit, to excel him in another.

But the condition of those who are absolutely miserable is more mysterious. What shall we say of those who are doomed to pain, imbecility, deformity? Exposed to suffering, unmerited ridicule, and disgrace, is it not excusable that they should envy their more favored neighbors?

Such distinctions are undoubtedly an occasion of coveting the possessions of others. Envy, however, is forbidden, and its wrongfulness can therefore be seen.

1. It is a useless passion. It does not tend to right action. Indeed it does not stimulate to

any action. It rusts and corrupts the soul that indulges in it. It adds to the pain of his deprivation an indescribable misery because another is happy.

2. It perverts the judgment. Under its influence an innocent person is hated simply because he is happy or prosperous. Unjust views of life are entertained. The good one really does enjoy is not properly prized. Few pause to reflect that such is the power of self-love that no person would be willing to exchange natures with another: why, then, should he envy another? And yet under the influence of envy he becomes sour, uncharitable, misanthropic. Were he cheerful and grateful he would find that he, too, had certain elements of character and certain sources of gratification that others do not enjoy. The rich man rolling along in his carriage looks out from the carefully closed window and sighs, "O that I had the health and strength and real enjoyment of yonder laborer;" the poor man sighs for the ease of the rich. Neither would exchange natures with the other, and if they should exchange, it is impossible for us to decide which would gain or lose. The least covetous would lose the most. True enjoyment is entirely independent of outward circumstances. It depends upon the proper and harmonious development and action of the mind, and upon a conscious harmony with the

will of God; and those who perhaps seek enjoyment least have it most abundantly. "A contented mind is a perpetual feast."

There is a peculiarity about this commandment that challenges attention. It differs from all statutes, ancient and modern, of a political character. It is not designed to regulate outward action but inward feeling. No penalty can be affixed to the breaking this commandment, to be enforced by human authority, for it can never be ascertained by man whether it is broken or not. Coveting is a process wholly internal, and yet it is forbidden.

This is one of those peculiarities of the Bible in which the handwriting of the All-wise One is conspicuously seen. Whence had Moses this philosophic, superhuman shrewdness? He had before him a nation of freed slaves; a horde of lately emancipated bondmen, so ignorant and so debased in their tastes and habits, that during an absence of a few days from them they forced Aaron to make them a golden image of a calf, and fell down before it with superstitious worship, and howled around it in miserable dances and songs. Their whole course proved them to be destitute of culture and thought. And yet Moses publishes to them this sublime Decalogue, beginning with the revelation of the proper object of worship, the One Great God, condensing into a few precepts the whole duty of man, and concluding with a precept directed to the heart, which cannot be positively obeyed without a heart full of love and resignation to the divine will. Whence had Moses this wisdom?

The Decalogue which we have thus briefly examined is condensed still further, by Him who spake as never man spake, into two precepts: "Thou shalt love the Lord thy God with all thy heart, with all thy mind, and all thy strength; and thou shalt love thy neighbor as thyself." We have the authority of Christ for the statement that this is the substance of all that is taught by the law and the prophets. The Old and New Testaments together aim only to induce men to do thus. The doctrine of atonement, of regeneration and prayer, the various usages of the Church, and the practices of religious life, are all valuable only as they conduce to this, and if they seem to interfere with it are perverted, and wrested into implements of destruction rather than of life.

This Decalogue can never become obsolete. It was designed for all men; and, obeyed, would render all men noble and worthy of immortal blessedness. It is a kind of concentration of the moral teachings of the Bible.

Who can gaze upon this Bible and upon its effects without astonishment and praise to God for his gift to man? A revelation was necessary to man. Human history, outside of the conservative influences of God's revelation, has invariably exhibited a sad tendency to degenerate. Popular instincts have always a substratum of truth, and the universal popular instincts in non-christian nations have recognized a tendency to degenerate. The gradual subsidence from the golden, down through the silver, into the brazen and iron ages, was a common thought in Greece and Rome. They might have added, prophetically, an age of mud and filth, for this only can describe the rottenness of society when Jesus came. The instincts of all heathen literature are the same. The facts in all human history show the same tendency. Primitive simplicity, temperance, frugality, longevity, virtue; subsequent ambition, despotism, substitution of outward police for inward principle, superstition, feebleness, disorganization, and depopulation, savagism. Such is the story of Egypt; such is the story of ancient cities and empires in Asia; such is the story, so far as it goes, of Southern Europe; such is the story of ancient Mexico; and such the dim traditions, confirmed by mysterious mounds and sepulchral remains, of the Indian of our own forests. It had passed into an historical axiom that nations have their growth and decay; and almost into another, that no nation once fallen is ever redeemed. What, then, was before the world but Malthusian desolation and death?

Now we look upon these theories as truth, as granite, inexorable truth. The deductions of heathen philosophers were right, so far as their vision extended, and they had no hope. Heathen philosophy did not try to stem the current of desolation with its baby hand. It yielded and wailed and satirized, and plunged into the same wickedness and woe, and went down laughing and cursing into the same abyss. It could do nothing else.

God has tried two grand experiments on the earth. The one was before the deluge, when men were intrusted with the pure religion, a virgin earth, long and vigorous life, and bidden to show their nature.

The result of the experiment was the catastrophe which justly washed the offensive mass away, and once more sweetened the earth and heavens. The second experiment was after the deluge, when the elements, more mixed and shorter-lived, seemed hastening to a similar result. But the universal destruction once more threatened was arrested by a sovereign remedy. Multitudes of smaller deluges had begun to destroy guilty man. Sodoms, Gomorrahs, Canaans, Babylons, and Ninevehs had fallen. But God had promised preservation. The world having exhibited, fully enough to convince the most skeptical, the incompetency of human nature to sustain itself, a new element was introduced. In the chemistry of the Omniscient a new ingredient was required. It is the Bible. It is the counter power of man's degeneracy. It is the bulwark of society. It is to restore the world to sweetness, man to reason, life to harmony.

Behold now the wisdom of God in the *shape* of the remedy he has provided. It is a Book. The nucleus of it all is the Decalogue—the first writing, the oldest of books—the autograph of God! Around this have clustered other writings, constituting a Book of books!

This Bible proves its own divinity by its comprehensiveness and its power. It is proved that the blood circulates through the whole body by the fact that you cannot anywhere make a slight puncture without drawing a drop, and in like manner the nervous energy must be everywhere, for everywhere is sensation; so the Bible permeates all history. Its facts constitute history, some of the weightiest parts, and absolutely indispensable parts. Therefore, whoever would know the past is compelled to face its facts and study them.

Who is not familiar with this impudent objection of infidelity—the Bible may have been a revelation to those who first received it, but to us it has no foundation but fallible, human testimony? The miracles may have been authoritative once, but they now encumber the record, and need to be proved themselves! Have not some sincere Christians feared that this Gospel, which is peace and joy to them, may to their children's children lack the outward evidence which their reason will demand? Give such fears to the winds. God will take care of his TRUTH. It is the truth only that we want. The expanded universe without and the spiritual teachings of the Bible within will mutually sustain each other. God furnishes to each age its own food for faith, and support of the truth. When miracles were needed men had them; when a higher and more spiritual evidence can be appreciated, that will not be wanting. History, too, will utter her thousand voices to confirm the truth, and prophecy piles up the record as it is translated into fact.

But the Bible alone will not save the world. There are three external agencies to accomplish this end. Just as there are three chords in music, three colors in the sun-ray, three agencies in light, three graces—Faith, Hope, Charity—so are three great external powers to sanctify and regulate humanity: the BIBLE, the MINISTRY, the CHURCH. Neither can long be vital without the other two; all together are Omnipotence and Love.

Be it ours, then, to obey the law, and enjoy the comforts of the Gospel; and having ourselves imbibed the spirit of the Bible, labor to bring about the time when every human being shall understand the Scriptures, every hamlet and company of men have a preacher of the Gospel, and the whole world embrace the Church of Christ.

THE END.

www.ingramcontent.com/pod-product-compliance
Lightning Source LLC
LaVergne TN
LVHW012328100826
845148LV00017B/397